THE GENIUS OF LANGUAGE

D0869828

[VII]

FOUNDATIONS OF WALDORF EDUCATION

RUDOLF STEINER

THE

GENIUS

OF

LANGUAGE

Observations for Teachers

SIX LECTURES
(*with added notes*)

Given to the Faculty
of the Waldorf School in Stuttgart, Germany
from December 26, 1919 to January 3, 1920

Translated by
Gertrude Teutsch and Ruth Pusch

Anthroposophic Press

*The publisher wishes to acknowledge the inspiration
and support of Connie and Robert Dulaney*

The lectures in this book are a translation of
Geisteswissenschaftliche Sprachbetrachtungen (GA 299),
published by Rudolf Steiner Verlag, Dornach, Switzerland, 1981.

Published in the United States by Anthroposophic Press
RR 4 Box 94-A1, Hudson, NY 12534

Library of Congress Cataloging-in-Publication Data

Steiner, Rudolf, 1861–1925.
   [Geisteswissenschaftliche Sprachbetrachtungen. English]
   The genius of language : observations for teachers; six lectures, with added
notes / Rudolf Steiner : translated by Gertrude Teutsch and Ruth Pusch.
     p cm. — (Foundations of Waldorf Education)
   "Given to the faculty of the Waldorf School in Stuttgart, Germany, from
December 26, 1919 to January 3, 1920."
   Includes bibliographical references and index.
   ISBN 0-88010-386-8 (alk. paper)
   1. Language and languages.   2. Language and languages—Religious
aspects. 3. German language—Semantics. I. Title. II. Series.
BP595.S85164413 1995   94–44037
299'.935—dc20   CIP

10 9 8 7 6 5 4 3 2 1

Printed in the United States of America

CONTENTS

isolation. Differentiations of language according to geographical conditions. Consonant shifts (1500 B.C.–500 A.D.); three language steps: Greco-Latin to Anglo-Saxon to German. The folk soul element: expletives. Inner wordless thinking.

Elements from the past in our own words. Earlier musical qualities of language now abstract, with no connection to our feeling life. The emotional, perceptive characteristic of language should be fostered. Shifts of meaning.

Use of language in the Middle Ages: nuances of feeling. Shifts of word meanings. The gradual separation of sound-perception and meaning (concept). Hazy sense of reality expresses itself in abstract language.

Elements of our feeling life and our will expressed by vowel qualities of words. Three steps of language development: consonants, vowel formation, reappearance of consonant emphasis. Concrete advice for teachers.

To one who understands the sense of speech
The world unveils
Its image form.

To one who listens to the soul of speech
The world unfolds
Its true being.

To one who lives in the spirit depths of speech
The world gives freely
Wisdom's strength.

To one who lovingly can dwell on speech
Speech will accord
Its inner might.

So I will turn my heart and mind
Toward the soul
And spirit of words.

In love for them
I will then feel myself
Complete and whole.

RUDOLF STEINER

Translated by Hans and Ruth Pusch

[This verse was given to the teacher of Greek and Latin, at the inauguration of High School classes in the first Waldorf School, Stuttgart, November 1922. Teacher and students were to speak it together at the beginning of class.]

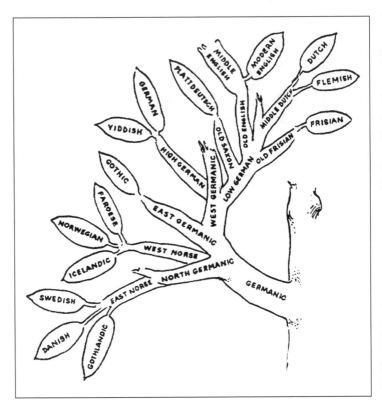

PART OF THE GREAT TREE OF INDO-EUROPEAN LANGUAGES
(Note: Old English is also known as Anglo-Saxon.)

In the beginning we are babblers. We are also citizens of the world, for during that first year of life we try out—at first tentatively and then uproariously—every sound and sound combination used anywhere in the world. We experiment with soft vowels, necessary for Polynesia; dramatic consonants, ready for the Czech Republic; sounds that are heard only in furthest Mongolia; even, perhaps, tongue-clicking like the Bushmen of the Kalahari Desert. None of them gives us any trouble. At the beginning we are geniuses of language.

However, our babbling leads us through syllables to words. We begin to *name* the beloved, necessary presence that is mama or mami or ma-ma-ma, reaching out to her and to the others around us. The world begins to become *our* world; with our mother tongue we become citizens of a fatherland. Speech has now a social character. In our naming there is an immediate understanding of word and meaning; sound and object are one. How could our Mama be any other person, or Dog any other dog? "Adam gave names to all cattle and to the fowls of the air and to every beast of the field." We were still in Adam's paradise.

Karl König tells us, "At this stage, speech awakens to itself and begins to unfold.... The child plays with speech and its words as if with the most beautiful golden balls that are thrown to him to possess."[1] Rudolf Steiner's references to the "Genius

---

1. Karl König, *The First Three Years of the Child* (Spring Valley, NY: Anthroposophic Press, 1969), p. 39.

of Language" in the six lectures contained in this book urge us to realize the transcendent quality of the realm of speech. A delicate echo sounds through the mysterious phrase: In the Beginning was the Word.

In his many lectures on language[2] Rudolf Steiner added a further dimension to the speech process. The first step of the continuing metamorphosis during a child's first three years, he pointed out, is actually the transformation of the baby's gestures and movements of the limbs into the movements of the larynx, bringing forth sounds of speech. This is a matter of hard work cheerfully undertaken by those small creatures—even the totally deaf—in their first year. The next step, during the second and third years, is what many child psychologists now recognize as the "internalizing of the language for the processes of thinking." König gives a remarkable image of this: "Speech is the plough that works the field of the soul so that the seeds of future thought achievement can be laid into the open furrows."[3]

A similar metamorphosis in the development of language belongs to the history of humankind as a whole. Gesture language came before spoken language. Consonants describing happenings of nature preceded vowels that gave voice to inner feelings. Words with a physical meaning (grasp, gather, figure, weigh, for instance) became abstract. We *grasp* an idea today far more often than we do a hammer or axe. Imaginative phrases ("glued love," "kingly legs") have fallen out of use.

Rudolf Steiner gave the lectures in this book to the teachers of the first Waldorf School, which had been established under his guidance for the children of factory workers in 1919. His

---

2. For instance, see Rudolf Steiner, *Education and Modern Spiritual Life*, Lecture 6 (Steinerbooks, Garber Communications, Blauvelt, NY, 1989).
3. König, op. cit.

words were not intended merely to give a foundation for the language classes[4] in the school—which of course they did—but more importantly, to encourage every single teacher in the faculty to work with language, enliven their classes with it, and bring the children to reverence for its place in life. This, certainly, is an ever-increasing task for all Waldorf schools.

Gertrude Teutsch, artist and art teacher in San Diego, California, first translated these lectures for the use of the teachers at Highland Hall, a Waldorf school in Los Angeles. It was a gifted labor of love done on the fly and blessed with her own quirky humor as well as a firm understanding of language development. A limited distribution reached the few Waldorf schools in existence in the early 1950s. Now there are over 100 Waldorf schools in this country and almost as many in the other English-speaking countries around the world. Many more are being founded every year, bringing their ideas and insights into the public schools as well. In this new publication the Language Lectures will be of far-reaching importance.

The English language, of course, has its deepest roots—its Anglo-Saxon heritage—in the old Germanic languages that reach back to the runes of the third century and the Gothic of Bishop Ulfilas of the fourth century. In this book, when Rudolf Steiner traces modern German words back to Gothic or Old High German, we realize that the same history can be followed back through north Germanic to Scandinavian languages or through west Germanic to Modern English and Dutch. We have tried to point out these common relationships, so that for

---

4. In 1919 the Waldorf School inaugurated the new and valuable method of beginning two foreign languages in the first grade, playfully at first, with enthusiasm and discipline carrying them through every grade of the elementary school. In high school one language is usually carried on alone. Greek and Latin are given in the fifth and sixth grades, but continued several years only in Europe.

our non-German speaking readers Steiner's examples will not seem at all exotic. He refers often to English words and the English language. The rules of the game, we find, are universal. *Whatever has been added by the translators is placed in brackets.* Single word or phrase translations are in single quotations.

May these printed pages begin to speak forth in ringing tones to every reader!

RUTH PUSCH
March 1994

Rudolf Steiner was asked to give these lectures to the Waldorf teachers in Stuttgart while giving the so-called Light-Course (GA 320).* Not only did he teach a scientific course with only a minimum of equipment, but he was also willing to improvise a course on language, requested by the teachers only on his arrival in Stuttgart.

In fact a third course is hidden in the second one—Steiner gave the secret away only at the end. The course as a whole can be seen as a demonstration, a practical introduction to teaching, a "Methods" course. In Steiner's characteristic way, it was flexible, expandable, alive.

I considered it a privilege to be able to make available to the teachers this work on a subject so close to my own heart. It was a translation "from the page into the machine." If it is now available in a more formal and permanent form, the thanks go to Ruth Pusch who has edited it, formulated the introduction, and has seen it through to completion. Due to her efforts, and skills, it will now be available to every language-lover. Thanks also are due to Christopher Bamford and Anthroposophic Press for seeing the value of this lecture series and undertaking the publication.

GERTRUDE TEUTSCH

*English edition issued by the Goethean Science Foundation, Clent near Stourbridge, Worcestershire, England, on behalf of the College of Teachers, Michael Hall, Forest Row, Sussex. Reprinted for the Steiner Schools Fellowship, 1977.

Language from an Historical Standpoint

SOME of our friends have asked me to speak about language while I am here in Stuttgart. At such short notice and with our limited time, this will have to be rather sketchy, certainly more so than with our scientific course. And you will have to have even more forbearance than you did for my remarks on "light," because what I say about language will simply be improvised. All I can do is to give you a few useful suggestions for your teaching here in the Waldorf School and also for teaching in general.

Perhaps we can find what we're after by first looking at some elements of language from an historical standpoint. Whatever I can bring together somewhat loosely today will be an introduction to further discussion during the rest of the time.

We can see especially in German how the development of a people's language expresses also the development of its soul life. We must keep clearly in mind, however, that the relationship of individuals to their own language varies from century to century. The further we go back in the history of a people, the more life we find in everything pertaining to language, within the forces of the human soul as well as in the pliant forces of the human body. I have often been aware of this; you will find as you go through my books a quite conscious attempt to use terms of Germanic derivation, even in philosophical matters.[1] This is frowned upon by many of my detractors, who condemn exactly what has been done very consciously with languages in my books. It is extremely difficult nowadays to find in German the inner, living forces able to continue forming the language. It is particularly difficult to find semantic correspondences by picking up some little-used word or extending the forms of a common one, as for instance I tried to do with the word *kraften* [The German noun *Kraft* 'force, strength' has only its corresponding adjective *kräftig* 'strong, robust'. Rudolf Steiner invented the corresponding verb *kraften* 'to work actively, forcefully' and the verbal noun *das Kraften* 'actively working force or strength'.] I tried with this to put action into what is usually expressed more passively. Other words I have also attempted, but—only one century since Goethe—it is already difficult to coin the far-reaching new words that will express precisely what we are trying to incorporate into our age as a new kind of thinking.

We can hardly remember that the word *Bildung* 'education, training, formation' goes back no further than the time of Goethe (1749–1832). Before that, there existed no educated (*gebildete*) people in Germany. That is, we did not speak of someone as *ein gebildeter Mensch* 'a person of culture, well-educated'. Even in the second half of the eighteenth century the German language had still kept a strong, sculptural vitality, so that it was possible to form such words as *Bildung* or even *Weltanschauung* 'world view', a term that also appeared after Goethe's time. One is indeed very fortunate to live in a language milieu that permits such new formations. This good fortune is evident when one's books are translated into French,

---

1. In German, we find two words for many things, as in English: *will* and *testament*, *send* and *transmit*, etc., one Germanic (Anglo-Saxon), the other Greco-Latin. In academic writing, the latter is usually preferred.

English, and other languages and one hears about the difficulties. Translators are working by the sweat of their brow as best they can, but always, when a person finishes something, another finds it horrible and no one else finds it any good. When you go into the matter more closely, it's clear that many things in my books simply can't be said in the same way in another language. I tell people: In German everything and anything is right; you can put the subject first or in the middle or at the end of the sentence—it will be more or less correct. The pedantic, dogmatic rule that something absolutely can't be said in a certain way does not yet exist in German as it does in the western languages. Imagine what we have come to when we're limited to stereotyped expressions! People cannot yet think as individuals but only in a sort of group spirit about the things they want to communicate to others. That is preeminently the case with the people of the western civilizations: They think in stereotyped phrases.

Actually, the German language in particular shows that what I would like to call the GENIUS OF LANGUAGE has gradually become rigid, and that German in our time is also approaching the state where we can't escape the stereotyped phrases. This was not so in Goethe's time and even less so in earlier ages. It is part of the picture of the whole language development in Central Europe.

Not so long ago this Central Europe, stretching far to the East, was still inhabited by a primitive people with great spiritual gifts but with a relatively simple outward culture, one that evolved substantially from trade and the economic life. Then roundabout, by way of the East Germanic tribes at first, much of the spiritual culture of Greece was absorbed. Through this, a great many Greek words entered the Germanic languages of Central Europe that later became modern German. During the centuries when Christianity spread from the South to the

North, its concepts, ideas, and images brought along an enormous quantity of vocabulary, because the Germanic tribes had no available expressions in their own languages for such things.

The word *segnen* 'to bless', for instance, is one of the words that came with Christianity. The specific concept of "blessing" did not exist in northern Germanic heathendom. There were indeed magic charms and they contained a magic power, but this was not of the same nature as a blessing. *Segnen*, the verb from the noun *Segen*, was taken into the language under the influence of Christianity; the word brought northward was *signum*, a 'sign'. Do observe what the genius of language still possessed at that time: language-forming strength! Nowadays we are no longer able to reconstruct and rework an adopted word in such a way that *signum* could become *Segen*, a blessing. We would treat the adopted word as an unchanged import, because the force and vitality that once transformed and created from the innermost depths simply do not well up any more.

Many words we take as completely German are in fact intruders; they appeared with Christianity. Look at the word *predigen* 'preach'. It is none other than the Latin *praedicare*, which also means 'to preach'. It was still possible to reconstruct this word from inside out. We never had a genuinely German word for this Christian activity of preaching. You see, if we want to get to know the actual force in German that transforms the language, we must first pour it through a sieve to sift out everything that entered our Central European culture from other cultural streams. In many of our words you will hardly notice it. You speak about the Christmas festival, feeling a strong attachment to it. *Weihnacht* 'Holy Night, Christmas' is a genuine German word, but *Fest* 'festival' is Roman, a Latin word that long ago became a German word. *Fest* goes back to the time when, along with Christianity, the most foreign elements found their way into the language, but at the same time were so transformed that we do not have at all the feeling today that they are imports. Who in the world remembers now that *verdammen* 'condemn, damn' is a Latin word that has become good German? We have to sift a great deal if we want to get to what is really the German language proper.

Many things came in with Christianity; others have entered because out of Christianity the whole system of education developed. The subject matter for educating was taken over in exactly the form it had in the South in the Greco-Latin culture. And there were no Germanic words for what had to be communicated. Along with the concepts, the vocabulary had to be imported. This happened first in the "Latin school" (high school), then it moved down into the lower school, and so today the basis of our education, the *Schule* 'school', itself is an imported word. *Schule* is no more a German word than *scholasticism*. *Klasse* 'class' is obviously a foreign word. Wherever you look: *Tafel* 'blackboard'; cognate, *table* from *tabula*, *schreiben* 'to write'; cognate, *scribe* are imports. Everything pertaining to school entered our language from outside; it came—with education itself—with Latin or the Romance languages from the South.

All this is one stratum that we have to sift off if we want to study the character of the German language proper. Almost all the specifically foreign words must be lifted off, because they do not express what comes out of the German folk soul but have been poured over its real being, forming a kind of varnish on its surface. We have to look for what lies underneath the surface. For instance, if we look beneath the varnish for things pertaining to education; we find relatively little, but that much is distinctive: *Lehrer* 'teacher', for one, a genuinely original German word, as is the word *Buchstabe* 'letter of the alphabet'—*Buch* 'book' is derived from it. It takes us back to the staves or sticks thrown down in ancient times to form the letters or runes that made up the runic words. They were beechwood sticks (*Buche* = 'beech'). From this then came the *zusammenlesen* 'gathering together', from which comes *lesen* 'to pick up', as well as 'to read' and then the *Leser* 'reader', which became *Lehrer* 'teacher'. These are ancient Germanic formulations, but you see that they have a totally different character, leading us back everywhere to the soul life of that time in Central Europe. The old heathen ways and the Christian ways collided, and with them the two elements of language, the northern and the southern. You can imagine what a strong power of interpenetration must have existed within the German language during the first millennium after the Mystery of Golgotha, that it could accept Christianity as strongly as it did and be at the same time able to accept the words that expressed the most essential mysteries of Christianity.

With this import, however, only one layer has been described, leading us back into the very early times connected with the great Germanic migrations, when the first Romance language stratum worked its way into the German language. Later the Romance languages were again to exert their influence. We can observe a second stratum originating from the Romance languages through various occurrences but this time coming from the West. Beginning in the twelfth century and continuing into the eighteenth, French words were taken over continually, French words for which there existed concepts and feelings, but by means of which the concepts and feelings were also modified. I have jotted down a number of these words but cannot claim any sort of completeness, for these lectures are being improvised from memory. I have tried to take words that seem truly German: for instance, the word *fein* 'fine'. You won't find this word before the twelfth century; it came by way of *fin* from the French. Here you can see how the language-forming power in the thirteenth century was still strong enough to transform a word so well that it is felt today to be a genuine German word. Even a word like *Kumpan* 'fellow, companion', which has become very popular, is only an adaptation of *compagnon*, and a word we often hear nowadays, *Partei* 'political party' also immigrated at that time, as well as *Tanz* 'dance'. All these words have been in the German language only since the second invasion of the twelfth century, which I would like to call French: *Schach* 'chess', *Matt* 'checkmate', *Karte* 'card', *Ass* 'ace', *kaputt* 'broken', and so forth. It is quite remarkable how many words came into Germany from the West, from France, during the twelfth and through the thirteenth, fourteenth, fifteenth, and sixteenth centuries, all of them contributing to the language an element of lightness, of easiness, where the German had a more ponderous quality. Before this time what had been spoken in German areas had a fuller, more rounded character. In it one couldn't very well have expressed playfulness. It would have been quite easy to say, *Du bist ein kühner Held* 'You are a bold hero'—the German language could have managed that—but not, *Du bist ein feiner Kerl* 'You're a fine fellow'. That could not have been said earlier, for one needed the word *fein*. Other things would have been just as impossible without the invasion of the French elements.

From Italy, remarkably little reached the more northern areas until, at the time of the Renaissance, some words relating to music came; that was all. However, a third kind of invasion, though not so pervasive, came later by way of a detour through southern Germany and Austria, bringing such words as *bizarr* 'odd, eccentric', *lila* 'purple', [obviously related to *lilac*] which had not existed earlier in German, *Neger* 'negro', *Tomate* 'tomato', all imported from Spain. Now the introduction of foreign elements enters a new phase; it is obvious that the genius of language is no longer as flexible as it had been. These later words are much more similar to their originals. And finally, when the Germans reached the stage of admitting English words, things had become most unfavorable; this was actually not until the late eighteenth and the nineteenth centuries. Words came into the language that related mostly to outer affairs, but they remained practically the same as in English. The German language genius had by then lost its capacity to adapt and completely absorb into itself something new.

I have tried to point out how in early times the ability to accept and transform language was extraordinarily strong, especially within the Germanic languages and early German. Take, for instance, (and I want to emphasize this in particular) a word that is so German that even a person very sensitive to dialects can really not doubt its authenticity: *Riegelwand* for *Fachwerkwand* 'half-timbered wall'. *Riegel* . . . truly German, as the tongue tastes and pronounces it! And yet this word was not part of the German language until the time when Latin-Italian trained architects used the kind of materials that could construct the *Riegelwände*. Who is aware today that this word *Riegel*, so typically German, is nothing other than *Regel, regula* Latin: 'rule'. We would not be capable of such changes in our present language. We also think *Keller* 'cellar' is an original German word, but no! It is nothing but an adapted loan-word from the Latin *cellarium*. I can give you another totally German-looking word to show you how difficult it would have been if people had begun to weed out and eliminate all the foreign words, as certain movements some time ago wanted to do. If that had happened, *Riegel* would have fallen by the wayside, *Keller* would have fallen—but do you know what other word would have had to go? *Schuster* 'shoemaker'! As a matter of fact, *Schuster* came into the German language because people from the South taught the Germans to *sew* their foot-coverings instead of tying them together. The Latin *sutor* (cf.

English: *suture*) refers to the sewing of footwear and has been assimilated into *Schuster*, an all-out foreign word.

You can see from this that we really have to sift vigorously to arrive at words of true German origin. We can not just accept what is floating nowadays on the surface of language, for this follows totally different laws. When we want to go back to the true speech-creating forces out of the genius of language, we must first of all sift off what is extraneous. The forming of language takes its course in a peculiar sort of way. You can see this very well by observing how things can still be introduced into a language—I would like to call it, through a certain kind of tyranny, from the bottom up—even when the language-forming genius no longer possesses its full strength. Not so many years ago, for instance, the following took place in Central Europe. Close to Raab there is a small town called Kocsi [now Kocs in Hungary]. I believe it was in the sixteenth century that an inventive fellow in this small place near Raab got the idea of building practical wagons that became very popular for people to drive and ride in. They made the little town well known. And just as Frankfurt sausages are known as 'frankfurters', these wagons were called *kocsi*. Just think how much carrying force was alive in this word, which grew into *Kutsche* 'coach'; it traveled to France and even reached the proud English! Yet this word is not especially old; it has moved in relatively recent times with a certain dynamic power in all directions from the wagonmaker in Kocs.

So let us understand this clearly: When we deal with a language already formed, we must remove many outer layers in order to reach the kernel proper. If we do reach this innermost part, we have to say: This kernel shows us without a doubt that it could develop with inner, language-forming strength only at the time when thoughts were much deeper and more substantive than they are, for instance, in German culture today. For this to happen, thoughts must be much more inherent in the whole human being. At the present time we can no longer feel that the force we perceive in our thoughts is also present in our words.

Sometimes we feel this force when we go back to the dialects that are to be found at a deeper, earlier stage of the language. At present, to express quickness we say *Blitz* 'lightning'. In certain southern German dialects the word is still *Himmlizer*. When you say that, you have the whole *Blitzform* 'shape of the lightning' in it: [*Himmel* is 'heaven'; —*lizer* reminds one of *licht*, 'light']. In this word there is a visualization of what takes on form in nature. In short, dialects still reach back to word-forms within which there is an echo of the happenings outside us in nature. This is always the case in the inmost kernel of a language, where the conceptual or ideational element is much closer to the element of sound. Through the history of the German language in particular we can observe how in earlier times, before language became abstract, it was still a matter of course that the meaning of words was imbedded in their sound. I would like to call it *a penetration of sense into sound*. A sensitive person can still feel it in such words as *Tag* 'day'; Anglo-Saxon, *daeg*, a truly original, ancient German word—can feel it in the /t/ and /a:/ (/ah/) sounds, especially through the help of eurythmy. Words that came later were formed out of abstract ideas. Look at the rather modern given name *Leberecht* 'live-right'. Parents endow a child with such a name in order to guide him or her with certainty along a virtuous path in life. There's also *Traugott* 'trust-God'. When such words came about, a certain language-forming element still existed but it was abstract, did not arise from a genuine inner source.

I wanted to say all this today as a preparation, so that we can proceed toward more concrete concepts and examples of language.

The Evolution of Language
from an Organic Point of View

I WOULD like to repeat what I told you yesterday: Please don't expect too much content from this very brief language study. I will make only a few remarks about the development of language in this improvised course. However, it is certainly worthwhile to stir up some thoughts on the subject, and perhaps from the way I present things, you will discover guidelines. I won't go into the usual facts, but I will try to show you a number of important ways to look at the life of language with a view to its organic evolving.

In my first lecture I referred to the development of our German language through "invasions" into its word-stock. We pointed to the significant one, which coincided with the streaming in of Christianity into northern cultures, and its consequences. Christianity did not simply bring in its own content; it brought this content in the form of word images. Considered outwardly, the folk religions of the northern and central European peoples were not at all similar to what came to them as a new religion; nor was it possible for them to grasp the content of Christianity with the words and sounds of northern and central Europe. Therefore, those who brought Christian concepts and Christian perceptions also brought their "word clothing." We have cited a group of such words that were carried northward, we can say, on the wings of Christianity. In the same way, everything connected with schooling streamed northward, too, words like *Schule* 'school' itself, *Tafel* 'blackboard', and so forth, with the exception of a few like *Lesen, Buchstabe, Lehrer* (see Lecture 1, pages 19–20). The former are of Latin origin, but have been integrated into the German language organization so thoroughly that no one today would recognize them as loan-words. I also described how later, beginning in the twelfth century, a new invasion arrived from the West, bringing in many language elements. After that came a Spanish wave and finally one from England, as late as the nineteenth century.

These examples will be elaborated on later, but they indicate that during the time Christianity and everything related to it were making their way northward, the genius of the language was still able to accept and transform it inwardly by means of the folk sensitivity in that region. I illustrated this unique fact not by a word pertaining to Christianity but by the connection of the word *Schuster* 'shoemaker', which seems so truly Germanic, with *sutor*: it is one and the same word (page 22–23). There was still so much speech-forming strength in the genius of the Germanic folk that it was possible to transform a word like *sutor* that belongs to the earliest invasion. The further we proceed from this to the next invasion, which was concerned with education, the more we find the sound of the word in German closer to the sound in Latin. And so it continued. Languages flowing in later found the German language spirit ever less capable of transforming whatever came toward it. Let us keep this in mind. It remains to be seen whether, in due time, such phrases as *five o'clock tea* will be changed; that is, whether the German language genius can develop over a relatively long span of time the power of more rapid transformation it possessed in early times. We will have to wait and see. At the moment, it is not important.

We must ask ourselves what significance it has for a people that its language-forming power is decreasing, at least temporarily; that in fact it no longer exists as it once was. You do find it more strongly today in dialects. For instance, we could search for the origin of a very strange word in the Austrian dialect: *pakschierli* or *bakschierli*. The Austrians sitting here certainly know it. You can quickly sense what *pakschierli* means: 'a cunning little girl who bobs and curtseys when presented to strangers', a 'charming little girl'—that's *pakschierli*—or a 'funny little thing made of marzipan' that doesn't exactly make you laugh, but causes an inward state of being ready, if the impression you get grows a little, to burst out in a loud laugh. 'A funny little thing made of marzipan'—that's *pakschierli*. Now what is this word? It is not really connected with the rest of the Austrian dialect, for it is none other than the German word *possierlich* 'funny, cunning, cute', a word that has been transformed.

In a way, then, this language-forming power can be studied in the dialects. It is also a good approach to the active, creative folk soul, and an understanding of the folk soul would contribute immeasurably toward an understanding of the cultural life of a country. It would lead back to what I referred to in *The Spiritual Guidance of the Individual and Humanity*,[1] which was ridiculed by such minds as the all-too well-known Professor Dessoir.[2] Spiritual science makes it possible to determine clearly what I described there: that the formation of consonant sounds in language is connected to an imitation of something externally perceptible. Consonants express for us what we have experienced inwardly of outside events. To put it more graphically: If you are

---

1. Rudolf Steiner, *The Spiritual Guidance of the Individual and Humanity* (Hudson, NY: Anthroposophic Press, 1992).
2. Max Dessoir (1867–1947). Author, *Von Jenseits der Seele: Die Geisteswissenschaft in kritischer Betrachtung* (Stuttgart, 1917).

setting in a fence post, you can feel this action inwardly by bearing down (*aufstemmen*, as 'stem' for skiers) on your foot. This is the perception of your own act of will. We no longer feel this inner act of will in the sound [št, pronounced sht] of *aufstemmen*, but in the early age of language development, you did feel in your acts of will an imitation of what was happening outside yourself. The consonant element has thus become the imitation of events outside the human being, while the vowel element expresses what is truly an inner feeling. 'Ah!' is our astonishment, a standing back, in a sense. The relationship of the human being to the outer world is expressed in the vowels. It is necessary to go back a long way in time if one wants to penetrate to these things, but it is possible to do so; then one arrives at the insight that such theories as the "bow-wow" or "ding-dong" theories are horribly wrong. They are incorrect and superficial. An understanding of the human being, however, can lead us toward discovering inwardly how a speech sound is connected with whatever we want to reveal of soul and spirit. Let us consider this as a question to ask ourselves, in order to find answers during the course of this study. In order to look rightly at the many and varied links in the chain of language, I will try to find characteristic examples to help us reach what we are trying to understand.

Today I should like to take some examples to show how language proceeds slowly from the concrete to the abstract. If we really want to study actual facts, turning to dialect again will be helpful. Let me mention one small example:

When Austrian peasants get up in the morning, they will say something about their *Nachtschlaf* 'night sleep' but not at all as you are apt to speak about it. You think of it basically as something quite abstract, for you are educated people. Austrian peasants are close to nature. To them, all that surrounds them partakes of spirit and soul, and they have a strong awareness of it. Even for them this is dying out now, but in the seventies and eighties of the last century, it was still very much present for anyone who, like me, wished to observe it. Even though peasants may still perceive the elemental forces in everything around them, they will never express it in abstractions but always concretely. A peasant will say, 'I have to wipe the night sleep (*Nachtschlaf*) out of my eyes!' To peasants the substance excreted from the eyes during the night that can be washed away, is the visible expression of sleep; they call it *Nachtschlaf*. To understand language that was still quite alive a short time ago, there is this secret: a factual understanding is not at all hindered by finding spiritual elements linked up with it. Austrian peasants are in fact thinking of an elemental being, but they express this by describing its action, that it put an excretion into their eyes. Never would they take this word as the abstraction arrived at by an educated person. However, if peasants have gone to school a little while or have been exposed to the city, they have a way of addressing themselves to an invisible, concrete fact. They will still say, 'I must wipe the night sleep out of my eyes,' but at the same time they will make a sort of gesture to imply that for them it is something really superficial and yet concrete.

We should be aware that such an observation leads us to realize that an abstract term always points back to something more concrete. Take the following example. In the Scandinavian countries you still find the word *barn* for 'child' [Scotland and northern England, *bairn*]; we no longer have it in German. What is its history? On one hand, it leads us back to the Gothic; we will find it in Ulfilas's Bible translation,[3] where we find the expression *bairan*, meaning 'to bear'. If we know the

---

3. Ulfilas or Wulfila (Little Wolf) 331–383. Bishop of the Goths. He is said to have invented the alphabet he used in order to translate the Bible. It is our only remnant of the Gothic language, which became extinct in 400 A.D.

law of consonant shift, discovered by Jakob Grimm,[4] for the
Germanic languages and for all those related to them [see lecture 3, page 41-42], we will go back from the Gothic *bairan* to
pherō in Greek and *fero* in Latin, both meaning 'to carry' or 'to
bear'. A /b/ in Germanic appears in Greek and Latin as /f/ or
/ph/. *Bairan* is simply a Germanic sound-shift from *fero*; the
word widens out into a different direction. There exists the
Old High German word *beran*, 'to carry' [*beran* is also the
Anglo-Saxon forerunner of English 'to bear'. The *barrow* of
'wheelbarrow' goes back to *beran*.]. Gradually the verbal aspect
of the word receded; in modern German we no longer have
the possibility of thinking back to the original, strongly felt,
active meaning. Why is the child called *barn* in Scandinavia?
Because it is being borne or carried before it comes into the
world. A child is something that is carried: we look back at our
origin. The only word left over from all this in modern German is *gebären* 'to bear, give birth'.

But we do have something else—we have retained the suffix
-bar. You will find that in *fruchtbar* 'fertile', *kostbar* 'costly',
'precious' and other words. What is *kostbar*?—that which carries a cost. What is *fruchtbar*?—that which bears fruit. It was
expressed very graphically, not as an abstraction as it would be
today, for the actual carrying, bearing was visualized.

You can imagine this quite vividly when you say something
is becoming *ruchbar* 'known', 'notorious', not always in the
most positive sense; literally, 'smell bearing'. When a smell is
being carried toward you, a matter is becoming *ruchbar*. For

---

4. Jakob Grimm (1785–1863), German philologist and creator of Grimm's
law. Interested principally in the relationship between the various Germanic
languages, he was one of the great founders of comparative philology. He
wrote *German Grammar, German Mythology* and—with his brother Wilhelm—the famous collection of German folk and household tales. The
Brothers Grimm also planned and inaugurated the great German dictionary.

many words like this we should be able to find the clear, direct imagery that in ancient times characterized the language-forming genius.

I will write down for you a phrase from Ulfilas's Bible translation:

jah witands Jêsus thôs mitônins izê qath

This means approximately, 'And Jesus, knowing their thoughts, spoke thus.' [Note *qath* = Anglo-Saxon, *cwaeth/ quoth*.] The word *mitonins* means 'thoughts' and this takes us to *miton*, meaning roughly 'to think'. In Old High German it grew into something different: *mezzôn*; related to this is the word *mezzan* which means *messen* 'to measure'. Measuring, the outer visible act of measuring, experienced inwardly, simply becomes thinking. Thus an action carried out outside ourselves has provided the foundation for the word *thinking*. 'I am thinking' actually means: 'I am measuring something in my soul'. This in turn is related to the Latin word *meditor* and the Greek *medomai*, which have given us 'meditate'.

Whenever we go back in time and observe the genius of language at work, we find this presence of imagery, but we must also try to observe it with inner understanding. You all know the term *Hagestolz* 'a confirmed bachelor'; you know its approximate meaning today. However, the connection of this word with what it meant formerly is very interesting. It goes back to the word *Hagestalt*, in which the word *Stalt* is embedded [modern German retained only the word *Gestalt*: 'figure, form, stature']. What is *Stalt*? It is a person who has been put, placed, or 'stood' somewhere. According to medieval custom, the oldest son inherited the farm; the younger son got only the hedged-in field, the *Hag*. The younger son, therefore, who only owned the *Hag*, was placed or 'stood' in this fenced-in field, and was often not able to marry. The *stalt* is the owner. The 'hedge' owner is the *Hagestalt*. As awareness of the word *stalt* gradually disappeared, people turned *stalt* into *stolz* (proud). It has no connection with the modern word *stolz* (proud); there is simply a resemblance of sounds. But an awareness of this *stalt* 'placed or stood' can be found in other, older examples still in existence, for instance in the Oberufer Nativity Play.[5] One of the innkeepers says *I als ein Wirt von meiner G'stalt, hab in mei' Haus und Losament G'walt* [I, an innkeeper of my stature—*or* an innkeeper placed here—take full charge in my house]. People think he means physical stature, but what he really means is 'placed in this respected house, *stood* here. . . .' With the words that follow, "Take full charge," he means that he attracts his guests. There is still the consciousness in *G'stalt* of what originally was in *Hagestalt*. We should follow with our whole inner being the development of words and sounds in this way, in order to ponder inwardly the unusual and delicate effects of the genius of language.

In the New Testament, describing how the disciples were astonished at Christ's healing of the man sick of the palsy, Ulfilas uses a word in his translation related to *silda-leik = seltsam-leich* 'seldom-like'. Considering the way Ulfilas uses this word in the context of his Bible translation, we discover that he means here—for what has been accomplished by Christ—*das Seltsamgestaltete* 'that which has been formed miraculously'. It is the bodily-physical element that arouses astonishment at this point. This is expressed more objectively in *silda-leik*. In the word *leik* we must sense: it is the *gestalt*, the form, but as an image. If the word *gestalt* were used in the earlier sense, it would be to express 'being placed'. The *form* (*Gestalt* today), as

---

5. A.C. Harwood, *Christmas Plays from Oberufer* (Bristol, England: Rudolf Steiner Press, 1993).

it earlier was felt, described the image of a thing and was expressed by *leik*. We have this word in *leichnam* 'corpse'. A corpse is the image of what was once there. It is a subtle expression when you sense what lies in this *Leich*, how the *Leich* is not a human being but the 'likeness' of one.

There are further examples I can bring you for the development of terms springing from visual imagery to express a quality of soul. We learn from Ulfilas that in the Gothic language 'bride' is *brûths*. This *bruths* in the Bible translation is closely related to 'brood' (*Brut*), so that when a marriage is entered upon, the *brood* is being provided. The "bride" is the one who ensures the 'brood'. Well then, what is the *Bräutigam* (the 'bridegroom')? Something is added to the bride; this is in Gothic *guma*, in Old High German *gomo* [in Anglo-Saxon, *guma*], derived by consonant shift from the Latin word *homo*, 'man', 'the man of the bride', the man who for his part provides for the brood [the addition of /r/ in the English *groom* is due to confusion with, or substitution of *groom*, servant]. You see, we have to look at the unassuming syllables sometimes if we really wish to follow the genius of language in its active forming of language.

Now it is remarkable that in Ulfilas's translation the Gothic *sa dumba* 'der Dumpfe', 'the dull one', appears, denoting the man unable to speak, the dumb man whom the Christ heals (Matthew 9:32). With this, I would like to remind you that Goethe has told us how in his youth he existed in a certain kind of *Dumpfheit* 'dullness'. "Dullness" is a state of being unable to see clearly through one's surroundings, to live in shadows, in fogginess; this hinders, for one thing, the capacity for speech, renders mute. Later this word became *dumm*, took the meaning of 'dumb' or 'stupid', so that this *dumb* means nothing more than 'not able to look about freely' or 'to live in dullness' or 'in a fog.' It is truly extraordinary, my dear friends,

how many changes and transformations of a word can exist.[6]
These changes and recastings show how the conscious and the
unconscious are interwoven in the marvelous being called the
genius of language that expresses itself through the totality of a
folk, tribe, or people.

There is, for instance, the name of the Nordic god *Fjögyn*.
This name appears in a clarifying light through Ulfilas's use of
the word *fairguni* as Gothic for 'mountain', in telling of Christ's
"going up into the mountain" with his disciples. Its meaning
shifted a little but we still find the word in Old High German
as *forha*, meaning 'fir tree' or 'fir mountain'. *Fjögyn* is the elemental god or goddess who resides on the fir mountain. This in
turn (and we can sense it in *fairguni*) is related to the Latin
word *quercus* 'oak tree', which also names the tree.

I should like to point out how in earlier ages of language-
forming there prevailed—though somewhat subconsciously—a
connection between sound and meaning. Nowadays it is almost
impossible for us with our abstract thinking to reach down to
the speech sounds. We no longer have a feeling for the sound
quality of words. People who know many languages are downright annoyed if they are expected to consider anything about
speech sounds. Words in general have the most varied transi-
tions of form and meaning, of course; translations following
only the dictionary are artificial and pedantic. First of all, we
should follow the genius of language, which really has something other in mind than what seems obvious at first glance.

In German we say *Kopf* 'head'; in the Romance languages it
is *testa, tête*. Why do we say *Kopf*? Simply because in German
we have a sculptural language genius and we want to express the
roundness of the head. *Kopf* is related to *kugelig* 'spherical', and

---

6. See also Rudolf Steiner, *Spiritual Relations in the Human Organism*, lecture 2 (Spring Valley, NY: Mercury Press, 1984).

whether we speak of *Kohlkopf* 'cabbage head' or human *Kopf*, it has originated from the same language-molding process. *Kopf* expresses what is round. *Testa*, however, 'head' in Latin, denotes something in our inner being: testifying, ascertaining, determining. We always have to consider that things may be named from various points of view. One can still feel this—though it's possible to miss the details—if we try to trace our way back to older forms from which the present word originated. Finally we arrive far back in time when the genius of language was able to sense the spiritual life within the sounds themselves.

Who can still sense that *meinen* 'to mean' and *Gemeinde* 'community, parish' belong together? Nowadays this is difficult to perceive. In Old High German *Gemeinde* is *gimeinida*. If you look at a further metamorphosis to *mean* as an English cognate [Anglo-Saxon, *maenan*, 'to recite, to tell' and Anglo-Saxon, *gemaene*, 'common, general'], it is evident that *gemeinida* expresses what is 'meant' or 'arrived at' by several people in common; it derives strength from the fact that several people are involved. And this act of receiving strength is expressed by adding such a *prefix* as *gi*-[related to Anglo-Saxon *be*-, in *bedazzle*, *behold*, and so forth. In modern German *ge*- is the prefix of most past participles.].

We have to reach back and try to find the element of feeling in the forming of speech. Today when we say *taufen*, an ancient German word, 'to baptize', we no longer have a feeling for what it really is. We get more of a picture when we go back to Old and Middle High German, where we find *toufan, toufen, töufen* and find this related to *diups* [who can resist finding a connection to *dip*, Anglo-Saxon, *dyppan*?], and in Ulfilas's *daupjan* related to *daupjands*, the Baptist. We have in Old High German the close cognate *tiof*, in Modern German *tief* 'deep'—so there we have the relationship *taufen . . . hineintiefen . . . tauchen* 'dip in, dive in'. It is simply a dipping into the water.

These things should help us to look carefully at the language-forming genius. Observing changes of meaning is especially important. In the following example there is an interesting shift of meaning. 'Bread' was in Gothic *hlaifs*, Old High German *leiba*, Middle High German *leip*, Anglo-Saxon, *hlaf*, modern German *das Brot*. *Hlaifs/hlaf* has not retained the meaning 'bread'; it has changed into *laib/loaf*. It means now only the form in which bread is made; earlier it was the bread itself.

You can observe this change of meaning in the metamorphosis from Old English *hlaford* from the earlier *hlafweard*, 'bread keeper or guard.' The *hlaford* was the person who wards or guards the bread, the one you had to ask if you wanted bread, who watched over the bread, had the right to plant the field, make the bread, give the bread to those who were not freemen. And by means of a gradual transformation—the /h/ is lost—the word *lord* developed; 'lord' is the old *hlafweard*.

The companion word is equally interesting. Whereas *hlaifs* becomes 'loaf of bread', another word appeared through metamorphosis: *hlaefdige* in Old English. The first part of the word is again 'loaf of bread'; *dige* developed from an activity. If dough (Anglo-Saxon *dag*, Modern German *Teig*) is being kneaded, this activity is expressed in the word *dige*, *digan*, to knead dough. If you seek the person who carries out this activity, you will arrive at the wife of the lord. The lord was the bread-warden; his wife was the bread-kneader, bread-giver. The word 'lady' grew out of *hlaefdige*. In a mysterious way, 'lord' and 'lady' are related to the loaf of bread and show their origin as 'bread-warden' and 'bread-kneader'.

We must really try to grasp the difference between our modern abstract attitude toward language and one that was truly alive in earlier times. People felt then that speech-sounds carried in themselves the spirit qualities, the soul qualities, that human beings wanted to communicate.

The Transforming Powers of Language in Relation to Spiritual Life

T H E experiences of life often lead to apparent contradictions. However, it is just when we carefully examine the contradictions that we discover deep and intrinsic relationships. If you ponder somewhat carefully what I explained in my first talk and restated in the second, and you compare this with my examples yesterday of the inner connections between European languages, you will find such a contradiction. Look at the two series of facts that were characterized. We find in modern German many linguistic "immigrants." We can feel how many words accompanied Christianity from the South and were added to the original treasure house of the Germanic languages. These words came to us together with Christian concepts and Christian perceptions; they belong today very much to our language. I spoke, too, of other immigrant words as significant because they belong to the widened range of our language possibilities, those that came in from the western Romance languages in the twelfth century. At that time the genius of the German language still possessed the power of adaptation; it transformed in its own way what was received from Western Europe, not only as to sound but also as to meaning. Few people suspect, I said before, that the German word *fein* (fine) is really of French origin: *fin*, and that it entered our language only after the twelfth century.

I mentioned Spanish elements coming in at a later time, when German no longer had the same strength of transformation—and how this strength was totally at an end when English words entered the German language during the last part of the eighteenth but particularly during the nineteenth century. Thus we see words being continually taken over in Central Europe, from the Latin or from the Greek through Latin, or from the western Romance languages. Because of all this, we can say that our present vocabulary has absorbed foreign elements but also that our language in its very origin is related to the languages that gave it seemingly foreign components in later times.

We can easily establish the fact—not in the widest sense but through characteristic examples—that languages over far-flung areas of the earth have a common origin. Take *naus*, for instance, the Sanskrit word for 'ship'. In Greek it is also *naus*, in Latin *navis*. In areas of Celtic coloring you will find *nau*. In Old Norse and the older Scandinavian tongues you have *nor*. [In English there is *nautical, nautilus, navy, navigate*, and so forth]. It is unimportant that this word root has been thrown overboard [German has *Schiff*, noun, and *schiffen*, verb, as English *ship*, noun and verb]. Despite this, we can observe that there exists a relationship encompassing an exceedingly large area across Europe and Asia.

Take the ancient East Indian word *aritras*. We find the word later as *eretmón* in Greek and then, with some consonants dropped, as *remus* in Latin. We find it in Celtic areas as *rame* and in Old High German as *ruodar*. We still have this word; it is our *Ruder* 'rudder', 'oar'. In this way one can name many, many words that exist in adaptations, in metamorphoses, across wide language sectors; the Gothic, the Norse, the Friesian, Low German, and High German—also in the Baltic tongues, the Lithuanian, Latvian, and Prussian. We can also find such words in the Slavic languages, in Armenian, Iranian, Indian, Greek,

Latin, and Celtic. All across the regions where these languages were spoken, we discover that a primeval relationship exists; we can easily imagine that at a very ancient time the primordial origins of language-forming were similar right across these territories and only later became differentiated.

I did say at the beginning that the two series of facts contradict each other, but it is just by observing such contradictions that we can penetrate more deeply into certain areas of life. The appearance of such phenomena leads to our discovering that human evolution through the course of history has not at all taken place in a continuously even way, but rather in a kind of wave movement. How could you possibly imagine this whole process, expressed in two seemingly contradictory bodies of fact, without supposing that some relationship existed between the populations of these far-flung territories? We can imagine that these peoples kept themselves shut off at certain times, so that they developed their own unique language idioms, and that periods of isolation alternated with periods of influencing or being influenced by another folk. This is a somewhat rough and ready characterization, but only by looking at such rising and falling movements can we explain certain facts. Looking at the development of language in both directions, as I have just indicated, it is possible to gain deeper insights also into the essential nature of folk development.

Consider how certain elements of language develop—and this we will do now for the German language—when a country closes itself off from outside influences and at other times takes in foreign components that contribute their part to the spirit-soul elements expressed through language. We can already guess that these two alternating movements evoke quite different reactions in the spirit and soul life of the peoples.

On one hand it is most significant that a primordial and striking relationship exists between important words in Latin and in the older forms of the Central European languages—for instance, Latin *verus* 'true', German *wahr* 'true', Old High German *wâr* [in German /w/ is pronounced /v/. We have in English *verity, very,* from Old French *veras*]. If you take such obvious things as Latin, *velle* = *wollen* 'will' or even Latin, *taceo* 'I am silent' and the Gothic *thahan* [English *tacit, taciturn*], you realize that in ancient times there prevailed related, similar-sounding language elements over vast areas of Europe—and this could be proven also for Asia.

On the other hand, it is really remarkable that the inhabitants of Central Europe from whom the present German population originated, accepted foreign elements into their languages relatively early, even earlier than I have described it. There was a time when Europe was much more strongly pervaded by the Celtic element than in later historic times, but the Celts were subsequently crowded into the western areas of Europe; then the Germanic tribes moved into Central Europe, quite certainly coming from northern areas. The Germans accepted foreign word elements from the Celts, who were then their western neighbors, much as they later accepted them from the Romans coming from the South. This shows that the inhabitants of Central Europe, after their separate, more closed-off development, later accepted foreign language elements from the neighbors on their outer boundaries, whose languages had been originally closely related to their own.

We have a few words in German that are no longer considered very elegant, for instance *Schindmähre*, 'a dead horse'. *Mähre*, 'mare', is a word rarely used in German today but it gave us the word *Marstall* 'royal stables'. *Mähre* is of Celtic origin, used after the Celts had been pushed toward the West. [While English *mare* is in common usage, *nightmare* has a different origin: Anglo-Saxon *mearh*, 'horse'; *mere*, 'female horse'; Anglo-Saxon *mara*, 'goblin, incubus'.] There seems to have been no metamorphosis of the word, either in Central Europe or the West; apparently the Germans took over the word later from the Celts. In fact, a whole series of such words was taken over, for some of which the power of adaptation could be found. For instance, the name—which is really only partly a name—*Vercingetorix* contains the word *rix*. *Rix*, originally Celtic, was taken up by the Celts to mean 'the ruler,' the person of power (Gothic *reiks*, Latin *rex*). It has become the German word *reich* (Anglo-Saxon, *rice*, 'powerful', 'rich'), 'to become powerful through riches'. And thus we find adaptations not only from Latin but also from the Celtic at the time when the Central European genius of language still possessed the inner strength of transformation.

If the external development of language could be traced back far enough—of course, it can't be—we would ultimately arrive at that primeval language-forming power of ancient times when language came about through what I described yesterday as a relationship to consonants and vowels, a relationship of sound and meaning. Languages start out with a primitive structure. What then brings about the differences in them? Variety is due, for instance, to whether a tribe lives in a mountainous area or perhaps on the plain. The larynx and its related organs wish to sound forth differently according to whether people live high up in the mountains or in a low-lying area, and so on, even though at the very beginning of speech, what emerges from the nature of the human being forms itself in the same way.

There exists a remarkable phenomenon in the growth and development of language, which we can look at through examples from the Indo-European languages. Take the word *zwei* (two), Latin *duo*. In the older forms of German [also Anglo-Saxon], we have the word *twa* or 'two'. *Duo* points to the oldest step of a series of metamorphoses in the course of which *duo* changes to *twa* and finally to *zwei*. It is too complicated to take the vowels into account. Considering only the consonants, we find that the direction of change runs like this: /d/ becomes /t/ and /t/ becomes /z/, exactly in this sequence:

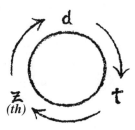

We note that as the word moves from one area to another, a transformation of the sound takes place. The corresponding step to German /z/ is in other languages a step to /th/.

This is by no means off-base theorizing. To describe the process in detail we should have to collect many examples, yet this sequence corresponds to Grimm's Law in the metamorphosis of language. [1]Take, for instance, the Greek word *thyra*, 'door'. If we take it as an early step, arrested at the first stage, we must expect the next step to use a /d/, and sure enough, we find it in English: *door*. The final change would arrive clockwise at /t/, and there it is: modern German *Tür*, 'door'.

Therefore we can find, if we look, the oldest "language-geological stratum," where the metamorphosing word stands on any one of these steps. The next change will stand on the following step, and then on the final step as modern German.

If the step expressed in Latin or Greek contains /t/, English (which has remained behind) will have the /th/, and modern German (which has progressed beyond English) will have a /d/ [cf. Latin *tu*, Anglo-Saxon *thu* 'thou', German *du* 'you'].

When modern German has /z/ (corresponding to English /th/

---

1. Jakob Grimm in his book on Germanic grammar codified this consonant shift so that it is known as Grimm's Law. See lecture 2, pp. 29–30.

the previous step would have been /t/, and the original Greco-Latin word would have had a /d/. This can be discovered.

We would then expect, following a word with a /t/ in Gothic, to find as the second step a /z/. Take the word *Zimmer* 'room', for the relationship of modern German to the next lower, earlier step in the Gothic or in Old Saxon, both of which stand on the same level: *Zimmer* has come from *timbar*. From /z/ we have to think back to /t/. This is merely the principle; you yourselves can find all this in the dictionary.[2]

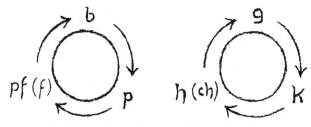

There are many other lively language metamorphoses; as a parallel to the just-mentioned sequence, there is also this one: if an earlier word has a /b/, this becomes on the next step a /p/, followed on the third step by /f/, /ph/, or /pf/ [Latin *labi* 'slip', Anglo-Saxon, *hleapan* 'leap', German *laufen* 'run'].

In the same way the connection /g/ → /k/ → /h/ or /ch/ exists. You will find corresponding examples [cf. Latin *ego*, Anglo-Saxon *ic*, Dutch *ik*, German *ich*]. We can sum up as follows: Greek and Latin have retained language elements at an early stage of metamorphosis. Whatever then became Gothic advanced to a later stage and this second stage still exists today, for instance in Dutch and in English. A last shift of consonants took place finally around the sixth century A.D., when language advanced one stage further to the level of modern German. We can assume that the first stage will probably be found spread far

---

2. See also Rudolf Steiner, *The Realm of Language* and Arnold Wadler, *One Language*.

into Europe, in time perhaps only up to about 1500 B.C. Then we find the second stage reigning over vast areas, with the exception of the southern lands where the oldest stage still remained. And finally there crystallizes in the sixth century A.D. the modern German stage. While English and Dutch remain back in the earlier second stage, modern German crystallizes out.

I urge you now to take into account the following: The relationship that people have to their surroundings is expressed by the consonants forming their speech, completely out of a feeling for the word-sound character. And this can only happen *once*—that is, only once in such a way that word and outer surroundings are in complete attunement. Centuries ago, if the forerunners of the Central European languages used, let's say, a /z/ on the first step to form certain words, they had the feeling that the consonant character must be in harmony with the outside phenomena. They formed the /z/ according to the outer world.

The next stage of change can no longer be brought about according to the outside world. The word now exists; the next stages are being formed internally, within human beings themselves and no longer in harmony with their surroundings. The reshaping is in a way the independent achievement of the *folk soul*. Speech is first formed in attunement with the outer world, but then the following stages would be experienced only inwardly. An attuning to the external does not take place again.

Therefore we can say that Greek and Latin have remained at a stage where in many respects a sensitive attunement of the language-forming element to the outer surroundings has been brought to expression. The next stage, forming Gothic, Old High German, Old English, and so forth, has proceeded beyond this immediate correspondence and has undergone a change to the element of soul. These languages have therefore a far more soul-filled character. We see that the first change that occurs gives language an inner soul coloring. Everything that enters our sensing of language on reaching this second stage gives inwardness to our speech and language. Slowly and gradually this has come about since 1500 B.C. This kind of inwardness is characteristic of certain ancient epochs. Carried over into later ages, however, it changed into a simpler, more primitive quality. Where it still exists today, in Dutch and English, it has passed over into a more elemental feeling for words and sounds.

Around the sixth century A.D. modern German reached the third stage.[3] Now the distancing from the original close attunement to the outside proceeds still further. Through a strong inward process the form of modern German proceeds out of its earlier stage. It had reached the second stage of its development and moved into the realm of soul; the third stage takes the language a good distance away from ordinary life. Hence the peculiar, often remote, abstract element in the German language today, something that presses down on the German soul and that many other people in the rest of Europe cannot understand at all. Where the High German element has been wielded to a special degree, by Goethe and Hegel for instance, it really can't be translated into English or into the Romance languages. What comes out are merely pseudo-translations. People have to make the attempt, of course, since it is better to reproduce things somehow or other rather than not at all. Works that belong permanently to this German organism are penetrated by a strong quality of spirit, not merely a quality of soul. And spirit cannot be taken over easily into other languages, for they simply have no expressions for it.

---

3. "Starting most probably in the southernmost reaches of the German-speaking lands, some time in the fifth century, a series of sound changes gradually resulted in restructuring the phonetic systems of all the southern and many of the midland dialects, resulting in High German"—John T. Waterman, *A History of the German Language* (Seattle: University of Washington Press, 1966).

The ascent of a language to the second step, then, is not only the ensouling of the language, but also the ensouling of the folk-group's inwardness through the language. The ascent to the third step that you can study especially in modern German [and especially in written German], is more a distancing from life, so that by means of its words such abstract heights can be reached as were reached, for instance, by Hegel, or also, in certain cases, by Goethe and Schiller. That is very much dependent on this reaching-the-third-step. Here German becomes an example. The language-forming, the language-development frees itself from attuning to the external world. It becomes an internal, independent process. Through this the human-individual soul element progresses which, in a sense, develops independently of nature.

Thus the Central European language structure passed through stages where from a beginning step of instinctive, animal-like attuning to the outer world, it acquired soul qualities and then became spiritual. Other languages, such as Greek and Latin, developed differently in their other circumstances. As we study these two ancient languages primarily from the standpoint of word formation, we have to conclude that their word and sound structures are very much attuned to their surroundings. But the peoples who spoke these languages did not stop with this primitive attunement to the world around them. Through a variety of foreign influences, from Egypt and from Asia, whose effects were different from those in Europe, Greek and Latin became the mere outer garment for an alien culture introduced to them from outside, essentially a mystery culture. The mysteries of Africa and Asia were carried over to the Greeks and to a certain degree to the Romans; there was enough power in them to clothe the Asian mysteries and the Egyptian mysteries with the Greek and Latin languages. They became the outer garments of a spiritual content flowing into them drop by drop. This was a process that the languages of central and northern Europe did not participate in. Instead, theirs was the course of development I have already described: On the first step they did not simply take in the spiritual as the Greeks had done but first formed the second stage; they were about to reach the third stage when Christianity with its new vocabulary entered as a foreign, spiritual element. Evidently, too, the second stage had been reached when the Celtic element made its way in, as I described earlier. With this we see that the spiritual influence made its entrance only after an inner transforming of the Germanic languages had taken place. In Greek and Latin there was no transforming of this kind but rather an influx of spirituality into the first stage.

To determine the character of a single people, we have to study concrete situations or events, in order to discover the changes in its language and its relationship to spiritual life. Thus we find in modern German a language that, on reaching its third stage, removed itself a good distance from ordinary life. Yet there are in German so many words that entered it through those various channels: Christianity from the South, scholasticism from the South, French and Spanish influences from the West. All these influences came later, flowing together now in modern German from many different sources.

Whatever has been accepted as a foreign element from another language cannot cause in us as sensitive a response as a word, a sound combination, that has been formed out of our own folk-cultural relationship to nature or to the world around us. What do we feel when we utter the word *Quelle* 'spring', 'source', 'fountain'; 'cognate, *well*'? We can sense that this word is so attuned to the being of what it describes, we can hardly imagine calling it anything else if with all our sensitivity we were asked to name it. The word expresses everything we feel about a *Quelle*. This was the way speech sounds and words were originally formed: consonants and vowels conformed totally to the surrounding world. [English speakers can feel the same certainty about *spring*: Anglo-Saxon *springan*. Arnold Wadler has pointed out the particularly lively quality of all *spr-* words, such as *sprout, sprig, sprite, spray, sprinkle, surprise*, even *sport*—and of course *spirit*.]

But now listen to such words as *Essenz* 'essence' or *Kategorie* 'category' or *Rhetorik* 'rhetoric'. Can you feel equally the relationship to what the word meant at its beginning? No! As members of a folk-group we have taken in a particular word-sound, but we have to make an effort to reach the concept carried on the wings of those sounds. We are not at all able to repeat that inner experience of harmony between word-sound and concept or feeling. Deep wisdom lies in the fact that a people accepted from other peoples such words in either their ascending or descending development, words it has not formed from the beginning, words in which the sound is experienced but not its relationship to what is meant. For the more a people accepts such words, the more it needs to call upon very special qualities in its own soul life in order to come to terms with such words at all. Just think: In our expletives and exclamations we are still able today to experience this attuning of the language-forming power to what is happening in our surroundings. *Pfui!* 'pooh! ugh!', *Tratsch!* 'stupid nonsense!', *Tralle walle!* [probably an Austrian dialect term. English examples: 'Ow!', 'Damn!', 'Hah!', 'Drat it!']. How close we come to what we want to express with such words! And what a difference you find when you're in school and take up a subject—it needn't even be logic or philosophy—but simply a modern science course. You will immediately be confronted with words that arouse soul forces quite different from those that let you sense, for instance, the feeling you get from *Moo!* that echoes in a "word" the forming of sounds you hear from a cow. When you say the word *Moo*, the experience of the cow is still resounding in you.

When you hear a word in a foreign language, a very different kind of inner activity is demanded than when you merely hear from the sound of the word what you are supposed to hear. You have to use your power of abstraction, the pure power of conceptualizing. You have to learn to visualize an idea. Hence a people that has so strongly taken up foreign language elements, as have the Central Europeans, will have educated in itself—by accepting these foreign elements—its capacity for thinking in ideas.

Two things come together in Central Europe when we look at modern German: on the one hand the singular inwardness, actually an inner estrangement from life, that results from moving into the third stage of language development; on the other hand, everything connected with the continuous taking-in of foreign elements. Because these two factors have come together, the most powerful ability to form ideas has developed in the German language; there is the possibility to rise up to completely clear concepts and to move about freely within them. Through these two streams of language development, a prodigious education came about for Central Europe, the education of INNER WORDLESS THINKING, where we truly can proceed to a thinking without words. This was brought about in abundant measure by means of the phenomena just described.

These are the things that have evolved; we will not understand the nature of modern German at all if we don't take them into account. We should observe carefully the sound-metamorphoses and word-metamorphoses that occur through the appropriation of foreign words at the various stages of development.

This is what I wanted to present to you today, in order to characterize the Central European languages.

History of Language
in Its Relation to the Folk Souls

YOU have seen that the most important concern of this course is to show how the history of language-forming originates in human soul qualities. Indeed, it is impossible to arrive at an understanding of the vocabulary of any modern language without understanding its inner soul nature. So I would like to add today some examples to show you how the phenomena of language are related to the development of the folk souls.

First let me call your attention to two words that belong together: *Zuber* 'tub' and *Eimer* 'pail'. They are old German words; when you use them today, you are aware that an *Eimer* is a vessel with a single handle fastened on top in which something can be carried; *Zuber* has two handles. That is what they are today when we use the two words, *Zuber* and *Eimer*. To investigate the word *Eimer* we have to go back a thousand years and find it in Old High German as the word *ein-bar*. You remember that I introduced you to the sound group *bar* (lecture 2), related to *beran*, 'to carry'. Through the contraction of *ein-bar* 'one carry', *Eimer* 'pail' came about. We have it clearly expressed, transparently visible in the old form: the carrying with one handle, for *bar* is simply something to carry with. *Zuber* in Old High German is *Zwei-bar* 'two-carry', a vessel carried by two handles, a tub. [The origin of *tub* from Middle

High German *tubbe* surely has to do also with 'two'.] You see how words today are contractions of what in the older form were separate pieces or phrases that we no longer distinguish.

There are many such examples; we can put our minds to a few typical ones. Take the word *Messer* 'knife'. It goes back to Old High German *mezzi-sahs*. *Mezzi* is related to *ezzan*, the old form of *essen*, 'to eat', with an introductory /m/. As for *sahs* (*sax* is another pronunciation of the same word), we need to remember that when Christianity spread across southern Germany, the monks encountered the worship of three ancient divinities, one of whom was *Sachsnot* or *Ziu*, the God of War [still present in English *Tuesday*, 'Mars-day']. *Sachsnot* means 'the living sword'; *sahs* has the same sound configuration. Therefore in the word *Messer* you have the composite 'eating sword,' the sword with which you eat.

Interesting, too, is the word *Wimper* ['eyelash' today, but seems to describe *eyebrow*], which goes back to *wint-bra*. *Bra* is the 'brow' and *wint* is something that 'winds itself around'. You can picture it: the 'curving brow'. In the contraction *Wimper* we no longer distinguish the single parts.

Another word that characterizes such contractions, where originally the relationships were felt perceptively, you know as the fairly common German word *Schulze* 'Mayor'. When we look back at Old High German we find *sculd-heizo*. That was the man in the village to whom one had to go to find out what one's debt (*Schuld*) was. He told a fellow who had been up to some kind of mischief what his fine would be. The person who had to decide, to say (*heissen*) what debt or fine was due was the *Sculd-heisso, Schuld-heisser* 'debt namer'. This became *Schulze*. I am giving you these examples so that you can follow me as we trace the course of language development.

Something else can be observed in this direction, something that still often happens in dialects. In Vienna, for instance, a great deal of dialect has been retained in a purer state than in northern Germany, where abstractness came about quite early. The Austrian dialect goes back to a primitive culture, as far back as the tenth century. The language-forming genius with its lively image quality was still active in southern German areas but did not enter the northern German culture. There is a picturesque word in Vienna: *Hallodri*. That's 'a rascal, a rowdy', who likes to raise a ruckus, who's a trouble-maker, who's possibly guilty of a few minor offences. The *Hallo* in the word points to how a person shouts [like English *Hello!* with a touch of *holler*]. The *ri* has to do with the shouting person's behavior; it is a dialect holdover from the Old High German *ari*, which became *aeri* in Middle High German, finally becoming weakened in modern German to the suffix *-er*. [This corresponds exactly to *-er* in English, as in *baker, farmer, storyteller.*] If you take the Old High German word *wahtari*, there at the end of it is the syllable you encountered in the Austrian dialect word *Hallodri*. It means somehow or other 'being active in life'—that is the syllable *ari*; *waht* is 'to watch'. The person who takes on the office of watching is the *wahtari*. In Middle High German it became *wachtaere*, still with the complete suffix. Now in Modern German it is *Wächter* 'watcher, watchman, guard'. The *ari* has become the syllable *-er*, in which you perceive very little of the original meaning: handling or managing something. This you should feel in words with the suffix *-er*, retained from ancient times, for example: The person who handles or manages the garden is the *gartenaere*, the *gardener*. It is an illustration of the way language today makes an effort to adapt sound qualities—everything I would call musical—slowly into abstractness, where the full sense of the sound can no longer be perceived, especially not in the full sense of the concept or its feeling quality.

The following is an interesting example. You know the prefix *-ur* 'original, archetypal' in the words *Ursache* 'first cause, original cause', *Urwald* 'primeval forest, jungle', *Urgrossvater* 'great-grandfather, ancestor', and so on. If we go back almost two thousand years in the history of our language, we find this same syllable in Gothic as *uz*. In Old High German, about the year 1000 A.D. we find the same syllable as *ar, ir,* or *ur*. Seven hundred years ago it was *ur* and so it remains today, having changed rather early. As a prefix to verbs it has become weak. We say, for instance, to express something being announced, *Kunde* 'message'; if we want to designate the first message, the original, the one from which the other messages arise, we say *Urkunde* 'document, charter'. In verbs the *ur* is weakened to *er*. To augment the verb *kennen* 'to know'; (cognate: *ken*) we do not say—as might have been possible—*Urkennen,* but rather *erkennen* 'to understand, recognize'. *Er* has exactly the same level of meaning in such a word as *ur* does in *urkunde*. If I make it possible for someone to do a certain thing, I *erlaube* 'allow' him something. If I change this into a noun, in a certain situation, it becomes *Urlaub* 'vacation', something I give a person through my act of 'allowing'. Another word formation related to all this is exceedingly interesting—you know the expression "to make land *urbar*" 'arable'. *Urbar* is also related to *beran* ('to bear'; see lecture 2). *Urbar* is the 'primordial cause inducing the land to bear'. There is an analogous meaning in the word *ertragen* '*ur*-bear, to yield, endure'. If you say nowadays something about the *Ertrag des Ackers* 'the yield of one's land', you are using the same word as in *urbar machen des Ackers* 'making the field yield its first crop'. Originally the word *urbar* was also used to say 'work the land so that it bears enough, for instance, to pay its taxes or rent'. [Note: English *acre* has become a measurement, whereas *Acker* is the land itself. Arnold Wadler in his *One Language* takes this word back to *Agros* (Greek, 'soil'), further back to *Ikker* (Hebrew, 'peasant'), and finally to A-K-R (Egyptian, 'earth-god') to show

how ancient words with a spiritual meaning descend through the ages to a sense that is more and more physical and abstract. 'God' → 'human being' → 'land' → 'measurement'. A similar change occurs from *Agni*, Hindu god of fire, to *Ignis* (Latin, 'fire') and finally *ignition*, 'part of an internal-combustion engine'.]

To study the prefixes and suffixes of a language is in every sense most interesting! For instance, there is the prefix *ge-* in numerous words. This goes back to the Gothic *ga*, in which one truly felt the *ga*thering. [Here the best example is offered in English: Anglo-Saxon *gaed*, 'fellowship', related to *gador* in 'together'.] *Ga-* carries the feeling of assembling, pushing together. In Old High German it became *gi*, and in modern German *ge* [Wadler once described the consonant as the musical instrument on which the vowel-melody is played, hence the ever-changing vowels in epochs of time and in comparable languages.] When you put *ge* in front of the word *salle* or *selle* 'room, hall', you come to *Geselle* 'fellow, journeyman' a person who shares a room with another or sleeps in the same lodging with him. *Genosse* 'comrade' is a person who *geniesst* 'enjoys' something together with another.

I want to call your attention to what is characteristic in these examples. Someone who experiences within the sounds of a word the immediate feeling for its meaning surely has a different relationship to the word than does a person without that feeling. If you simply say *Geselle* because you've known what it means since childhood, it is a different thing than if you have a feeling for the room and the connection within the room of two or more people. This element of feeling is being thrown off; the result is the possibility of abstractness.

Another example is part of many of our words, the suffix *-lich* (English *-ly*) as in *göttlich* 'divine, godly', and *freundlich* 'friendly'. If you look for it two thousand years ago, you will find it in Gothic as *leiks*. It became *lich* in Old High German, related originally to *leich* and also *leib* 'body'. I told you (see lecture 2, pages 32–33) that *leich/leib* expresses the 'form' (*Gestalt*) left behind when a person dies. *Leichnam* 'corpse' is really a some-what redundant expression, a structure such as a child creates when it combines two similar sounding words like *bow-wow* or *quack-quack*, where the meaning arises through repetition. Dis-similar sounding words, however, may also be combined in this way, and such a combination is the word *Leichnam*. *Leich*, as we said, is the form that remains after the soul has left the body. *Nam*, in turn, derives from *ham* and *ham* is the word still pre-served in *Hemd* 'shirt', meaning shroud or sheath, *Hülle*. *Leich-nam* means therefore the 'form-shroud' that we cast off after death. Hence there is a combination of two similar things, 'form' and—somewhat altered—'sheath', put together like *bow-wow*.

Out of this *leiks/leich* our suffix -*lich* has developed. When we use the word *göttlich* 'godly', it points toward a 'form' with its - *lich,* which is *leiks* 'form': a form that is godly or divine, 'of the shape or form of God'. This is particularly interesting in the Old High German word *anagilih*, which still contains *ana* from the Gothic; *ana* means 'nearly', 'almost'. *Gilih* is the *form*. Today's word *ähnlich* 'similar, analogous' means what 'almost has the form'.

This is a good example for studying not so much the history as more particularly the psychology of language. It still shows how nuances of feeling, in earlier times, were vividly alive in the words people used. Later this feeling, this emotional quality slowly separated from any language experience, so that what-ever unites a mental picture with speech sounds has become a totally abstract element. I have just spoken about the prefix *ge-*, Gothic *ga-*. Imagine that the 'gathering together' of *ga-*, which is now *ge-*, could still be felt and were now applied to the ele-ment of 'form', to the *leich*, then according to what we could feel historically, it could mean 'agreement of form'. This meaning lives in the word like an open secret. *Geleich* = *gleich* means 'forms that agree', 'forms that act together': *gleich* 'very similar, identical, equal'.

Consider for a moment a word that unveils many secrets. Today we will look at it from only one point of view. It is *Ungetüm* 'monster'. [In German the two dots over an /ä/, /ö/ or /ü/, called an *Umlaut*, change the quality and sound of the vowel.[1]] The /ü/ in *Ungetüm* was originally /u/ and this *tum*, if looked at separately, goes back to Old High German *tuom*, which is related to the verb *tun* 'to do, bring about, achieve, bring into a relationship'. In every word containing the suffix *-tum*, the relationship of things working together can still be felt—as in *Königtum* 'kingdom', *Herzogtum* 'dukedom, duchy'. The *Ungetüm* is a creature with whom no real working together is possible. *Un*, the prefix, denotes the 'negative'; *getum* could be the 'working together'.

We have numerous words, as you know, with the suffix *-ig* (English *-y*), such as *feurig* 'fiery', *gelehrig* 'docile, teachable', [cf. *saucy, bony, earthy*] and so on. This goes back to Old High German *-ac* or *-ic* and to Middle High German *-ag* or *-ig*. It signifies approximately what we describe with the adjective *eigen* 'own, one's own'. Hence, where the suffix *-ig* appears, it points to a kind of ownership. *Feurig* is *feuereigen*, something whose property is 'fiery'. I have told you that it is possible to observe how the genius of a language undergoes increasing abstractness, which is the result of this sort of contracting and what comes about then as the assimilation of sound elements, such as *feurig* from *feuer-eigen*.

It could be expressed like this: In very ancient stages of a people's language development, the feelings were guided totally

---

by the speech sounds. One could say language was made up only of differentiated, complicated images through the consonant sounds, picturing outer processes, and of vowel elements, interjections, expressions of feeling occurring within those consonant formations. The language-forming process then moves forward. Human beings pull themselves out, more or less, of this direct experience, the direct sensing of sound language. What are they actually doing as they pull themselves out and away? Well, they are still speaking but as they do so, they are pushing their speech down into a much more unconscious region than the one where mental pictures and feelings were closely connected with the forming of the sounds. Speech itself is being pushed down into an unconscious region, while the upper consciousness tries to catch the thought. Look closely at what is going on as soul-event. By letting the sound associations fall into unconsciousness, human beings have raised their consciousness to mental pictures (*Vorstellen*) and perceptions that no longer are immersed in language sounds and sound associations. Now people have to try to capture the meaning, a meaning somehow still indicated by the sounds but no longer as intimately connected with them as it had been. We can observe this process even after the original separating-out of the sound associations has taken place; just as people previously had related to the sounds, now they had to make a connection to words. By that time there had come into existence words with sound associations no one finds any relationship to; they are words connected through memory to the conceptual. There, on a higher level, words pass through the same process that sounds and syllables underwent earlier.

Suppose you want to say something about the people of a certain area, but you don't want to sound completely abstract. You wouldn't want to say "the human beings of *Württemberg*" [the German state where the lecture was being given]; that would be too abstract. And you probably wouldn't want to reach top level abstraction with "the inhabitants of Württemberg." If you want to catch something more concrete than "human beings," you might think of "the city and country people of Württemberg" (*die Bürger und Bauern*). This would denote not actually city people nor country people but something that hovers in between. In order to catch that hovering something, both words are used. This becomes especially clear and interesting when the two words, used to express a concept, approach from two sides and are quite far apart from each other, for instance when you say *Land und Leute* 'land and people'. [Something similar in English: *the world and his wife*.]. When you use such a phrase, what you want to express is something hanging between the two words that you are trying to approach. Take *Wind und Wetter* 'wind and weather': when you say it, you can't use just one word; you mean neither wind nor weather, but something that lies between, put into a kind of framework. [In English we have many similar double phrases from earliest times: *might and main*; *time and tide*; *rack and ruin*; *part and parcel; top to toe*; *neither chick nor child*— and many of them are alliterative, that is, repeating the same consonant at the beginning of both words.].

It is interesting to note that as language develops, such double phrases use alliteration, assonance, or the like. This means that the feeling for tone and sound is still playing its part; people who have a lively sense for language are still able, even today, to continue using such phrases and with them are able to capture a mental image or idea for which one specific word is not immediately available.

Suppose I want to describe how a person acts, what his habits are, what his essential nature is. I will probably hesitate to use just one word that would make him out to be a living person but passive—for I don't want to characterize him as living essentially a passive life nor on the other hand an active life; I want to deduce his activity out of his intrinsic nature. I can't say, his soul *lebt* 'exists'; that would be too passive. Nor can I say, his soul *webt* 'is actively in motion, weaves, wafts'; that would be too active. I need something in between, and today we can still say, *Die Seele lebt und webt* 'Just as he lives and breathes'.

Numerous examples of this kind proceed from the language-forming genius. If you want to express what is neither *Sang* 'song' nor *Klang* 'sound', we say *Sang und Klang* 'with drums drumming and pipes piping'. Or you might want to describe a medieval poet creating both the melody and the words of a song—people often wanted to say that the Minnesingers did both. One couldn't say *Sie ziehen herum und singen* 'they wander about and sing' but rather, *Sie ziehen herum und singen und sagen* 'they wander about singing and telling'. What they did was a concept for which no single word existed. You see, such things are only what I would call latecomers or substitutes for the sound combinations we no longer quite understand. Today we form contractions of such phrases as *Sang und Klang, singen und sagen*, sound-phrases which in earlier times retained the connection between sound-content and the conceptual feeling element.

To take something very characteristic in this respect, look at the following example. When the ancient Germans convened to hold a court of justice, they called such a day *tageding* 'day-thing'. What they did on that day was a *ding*. We still use the expression *Ding drehen*, literally, 'to turn a thing'; slang, 'to plan something fishy'. A *ding* is what took place when the ancient Germans got together to make legal decisions. They called it a *tageding*. Now take the prefix *ver-*: it always points to the fact that something is beginning to develop (Anglo-Saxon *for-* used in *forbear, forget, forgive*, and so forth). Hence, the occurrences at the *tageding* began to develop further and one could say, they were being *vertagedingt*. And this word has slowly become our *verteidigen* 'to defend, to vindicate', with a small change of meaning. You see how the sound combination *vertageding* began to undergo the same process as the word combinations do later.

Thus we find that little by little the conceptual life digresses ever further from the pure life of language sounds. Consider the example of the Old High German word *alawari*. *All-wahr, ganz wahr* 'completely true, altogether true' was the original meaning, but it has become today's word *albern* 'foolish'. Just think what shallowness of the folk soul you are looking into when you see that something with the original meaning of 'altogether true' has become 'foolish', as we hear and feel the word today. The *alawari* must have been used by tribes, I would say, who considered the appearance of human all-truth as something stupid and who favored the belief that a clever person is not *alawari*. Hence the feeling that 'one who is completely honest is not very clever', i.e., *albern*: 'silly, foolish, weak-minded'. It has carried us over to something for which originally we had a quite different feeling.

When studying such shifts of meaning, we are able to gaze deeply into the language-forming genius in its connection with qualities of soul. Take our word *Quecksilber* 'quicksilver, mercury', for instance, a lively, fluid metal. *Queck* is the same word as *Quecke* 'couch grass', also called 'quick, quitch, twitch, or witch grass', which has to do with movement, the same word as *quick* contained in the verb *erquicken* 'to refresh, revive'; cognate, *to quicken*, 'the quick and the dead'. This sound combination *queck* and *quick*, with the small shift to *keck* 'bold, saucy' originally meant 'to be mobile'. If I said five hundred years ago *'er ist ein kecker Mensch'*, I would have meant that he is a 'lively person', not one to loaf around, to let the grass grow under his feet, one who 'likes work and gets going'. Through a shift of meaning, this *keck* has become 'bold, saucy'. The path inward toward a soul characteristic led at the same time to an important change of meaning.

Another word *frech* originally meant *kühn im Kampfe* 'bold in battle'. Only two hundred years ago *frech* 'fresh, impudent, insolent' meant a courageous person, someone not afraid to stand his man in a fight. Note the shift of meaning. Such shifts allow us to look deeply into the life and development of the human soul.

Take the Old High German word *diomuoti*. *Deo/dio* always meant 'man-servant'; *muoti* is related to our word *Mut* 'courage'; cognate, *mood*, but formerly it had a different meaning, to be explained today by *attitude*, the way we are attuned to the world or to other people. We can say that *dio muoti* actually signified the attitude of a servant, the mood a servant should have toward his master. Then Christianity found its way north. The monks wanted to tell the people something of what their attitude should be toward God and toward spiritual beings. What they wanted to express in this regard they could only do in relation to the feeling they already had for the 'servant's attitude'. And so *diomuoti* gradually became *Demut* 'humility'. The religious feeling of humility derives from the attitude of a servant in ancient Germanic times; this is how shifts of meaning occur.

To study this process it is especially interesting to look at words, or rather the sound- and syllable-combinations where the shift of meaning arose through the introduction of Christianity. When the Roman clergy brought their religion to the northern regions of Europe, changes occurred whose fundamental significance can be outwardly understood only by looking at the shifts of meaning in the language. In earlier times before the advent of Christianity, there existed a well-defined master/servant relationship. About a person who had been captured in battle, put into service, and made submissive, his master—wishing to imply *Der ist mir nützlich* 'he is useful to me'—would say *Der ist fromm, das ist ein frommer Mensch* 'he is a pious man'. Only a last remnant of this word *fromm* exists today where, to put it a bit jokingly, it is only somewhat reminiscent of its original meaning in the phrase *zu Nutz und Frommen* 'for use and profit', that is, 'for the greater good'. The verb *frommen* is combined here with 'usefulness', which originally was its identical meaning, but the idea of finding something useful is pointed out with tongue in cheek. The servant who was *fromm* was a most useful one. The Roman clergy did find that some people were more useful to them than others and these they called *fromm* 'pious'. And so this word has come about in a peculiar way through the immigration of Christianity from Rome. With such words as *Demut* 'humility' and *Frommsein* 'piety' you can study some of the special impulses carried by Christianity from south to north.

To understand language and its development you have to pay attention to its soul element, to the inner experience that belongs to it. There exists in the forming of words what I characterized as the consonantal element on the one hand, the imitation of external processes, and on the other hand, the element of feeling and sensing, for instance, as interjections., when perceptions are expressed in their relationship to the external world. (See also expletives, lecture 3, p 48)

Let us consider a distinctly consonantal effect one can experience in one's feeling for language, quite far along in its development.

Suppose that someone is looking at this form I am drawing here. A simple person long ago would have had two kinds of feeling about it. Looking at the form from below, that person perceived it as something pressed inward; the feeling itself slowly grew into the sound formation we have in our word *Bogen* 'bow, as in rainbow'. However, looking at the form from above downward and perhaps bending it out as much as possible (drawing it), what I see now, looking down, comes into speech as *Bausch* 'hump, bunch, ball'. From below it is a *Bogen*; from above, it is a *Bausch*. The two words still contain something of our perceptive feeling. When you want to express what is contained in both words together but is no longer attached to our perception, and goes outward to describe the whole process, you may say *in Bausch und Bogen*, 'in bump and bow' ['lock, stock and barrel' is a similar English idiomatic phrase]. *In Bausch und Bogen* would be an imaginative phrase for this (pointing to the drawing), seen from above and below. You can apply these two points of view also in the moral or social realm, in closing a business deal with someone, so that the final outcome is considered from both inside and outside. Looking at it from within, the result is profit; from outside there is the corresponding loss. When you close a business deal, whether for profit or loss, you can say it's done *in Bausch und Bogen*; you don't have to pay attention to either of the single components (as in the English phrase *for better or for worse*).

With all this I have wanted to explain to you that by following the development of speech sound elements as well as words and phrases, pictures will arise of the folk soul development as such. You will be able to discover many things if you trace along these lines the movement from the concrete life of speech sounds to the abstract life of ideas. You need only to open an ordinary dictionary or pick up words from the talk going on around you, and then trace the words as we have done. Especially for our teachers I want to mention that it is extraordinarily stimulating to point out such bits of language history occasionally to the children right in the middle of your lesson; at times it can truly enlighten a subject and also stimulate more lively thinking. But you must remember that it's easy to get off on the wrong track; one must be exceedingly careful, for—as we've seen—words pass through a great variety of metamorphoses. It is very important to proceed conscientiously and not seize on superficial resemblances in order to form some theory or other.

You will see from the following example how necessary it is to proceed cautiously. *Beiwacht* 'keeping watch together' was originally an honest German word, like *Zusammenwacht* 'together watch', used to describe people sitting together and keeping watch. It is one of the words that did not wander from France into Germany as so many others did, but it somehow managed to wander into France, as did the word *guerre* (French, 'war') from the German *Wirren* 'disorder, confusion'. In early times *Beiwacht* got to France and there became *bivouac*. And then it wandered back again, in one of the numerous treks of western words moving toward German regions after the twelfth century. When it returned, it became *Biwak* 'an encampment for a short stay'. Thus an original German word wandered into France and then returned. In between it was used very little. Such things can happen, you see: Words emigrate, then it gets too stuffy for them in the foreign atmosphere—and back home they come again. There are many sorts of relationships like this that you can discover.

Language and
the Sense for Reality or Its Lack

ON the basis of what I have given you in these lectures and in order to reaffirm it strongly, I want to start out today with this remark: It is notably in philology that the consequences of a materialistic approach are the saddest, but perhaps also the most obvious. We can say that materialistic methods probably do more harm, for instance, in physics, because there it is less obvious—but it is most saddening in connection with language. Just here this could have been most easily avoided; just here it would have been possible to see how spirit and soul are actually at work in the language-forming genius. Now with this insight, our task will be to approach the earlier periods of language-forming by observing first of all what happens in later times. It is easier to survey the more recent happenings; you can follow language changes by noting how they shine through the accompanying changes in the feelings and perceptions of the folk soul. The language of the German people around the time of the Minnesingers—historians call it the age of chivalry—lies relatively far back but not so far that one can't trace literary matters easily enough to clarify this or that shift of meaning. By that time you don't find as many uncomplimentary phrases and epithets as in Homer, whose heroes applied names to each other that we would call insulting. Today we would hardly call each other 'goat stomachs' or 'donkeys'. In those ancient times, however, a donkey was held in such esteem that a hero could be called a donkey. Animals then, it is evident from the Homeric epics, were by no means the object of such nuances of feeling as they are today.

We can come to some understanding of these things if we look for characteristic examples from a time close to ours. In the Middle Ages we find the figure of speech: *Sie klebten wie ein Pech an ihrer Feinde Scharen* 'They stuck like pitch to the ranks of the enemy'. It sounds laughable today to say of a person who perseveres bravely in battle, 'He sticks like pitch', but this expression was definitely used in the age of the Minnesingers.

In Wolfram von Eschenbach[1] you will find a characteristic figure of speech, showing us first of all what was considered important at the time: description through vivid images, and secondly, various nuances of feeling for things or processes that would today seem rather contemptuous. When von Eschenbach describes in a serious manner a duchess coming toward a gentleman, he says, Her appearance penetrated his eye and entered his heart, *wie eine Nieswurz durch die Nase* 'like a sneezewort through the nose'. This is a vivid metaphor, for the scent of sneezewort penetrates one's nose in a very lively way, one could even say *ruchbar* 'smellable' (see lecture 2, page 30), but we would certainly not use the phrase today. It shows how the world of feeling has changed, and this change in the world of feeling must be studied in order to get at the science of language in a nonmaterialistic way.

A more recent poet,[2] as you know, was still able to say of a dignified woman, *Sie blickte wie ein Vollmond drein* 'Her glance

1. Wolfram von Eschenbach (1170–1220), German epic poet and knight. Most famous work: *Parzival.*

2. Ludwig Uhland (1787–1862) in "Des Sängers Fluch."

was like the full moon'. But this figure of speech, quite usual in the Middle Ages, would be inexcusable today. If you were prompted by a similar emotion to exclaim in this way to a lady, it would hardly be polite. In the Middle Ages, however, the loveliness and gentleness of the moon were transcendent in the hearts of the people. It was from this point of view that the association came about of the full moon with the beloved qualities of a lady's glance and countenance.

Gottfried von Strassburg speaks in his *Tristan*[3] quite seriously about *geleimte Liebe* 'glued love' as something that had come apart and then found its way together again. He spoke too about *klebenbleiben* 'staying glued down' of wounded men on the battlefield. This would sound insulting today. When people in the Middle Ages described the *kaiserlichen Beine* 'imperial legs' of a person in order to express his stateliness, or *die kaiserliche Magd Maria* 'the imperial maid Mary', it points up essential aspects of change within the world of feeling.

In bringing you these examples, I want you to become observant as to how these subtle changes of feeling show up in obscure areas. For instance, one could speak in those early ages of *krankem Schilfrohr* 'sick reeds'. What are sick reeds? *Krank*, 'sick', is here only a descriptive adjective for an exceedingly long, thin reed, and it is not at all far back in time when *krank* had no other meaning than 'slim'. In those days when you called a person *krank*, you would have meant that he was 'tall and slim', certainly not that he was 'ill', in the present sense of the word. Had you wished to express *sick*, you would have used the term *süchtig, von einer Sucht befallen*, in modern usage, 'chronically ill' or 'addicted'. To be *krank* was to be 'thin'—just think what has happened to this word! Gradually the feeling developed that it is 'not quite human' to be 'thin'. The notion has been adopted

---

3. *Tristan and Isolde*, ca. A.D. 1210.

that a normal human being should be a little more substantial. With this detour came about the linking of the sound-connection *krank* with the meaning 'sick' and the idea of a not-quite normal organism. We see how a word with one distinct shade of meaning can take on a clearly different one.

Not very long ago an innkeeper could do a good business by advertising *elenden* 'miserable' wine. He could trumpet forth in his village: "In my inn you get *elenden* wine!" It is exactly the same word that means 'miserable' today. Now, however, only in a dialect will you still find an echo of the old shade of meaning, where certain villages lying far out toward the border of the land are called the *Elend* villages. Even in my time in Styria in southern Austria, someone saying *Der Mann ist aus dem Elend* (the man is from the *Elend*) meant that he came from a village on the border. Certain villages have kept the name *Elend* up to the present day. This term has actually moved in from farther away, for *elender* wine meant *ausländischer* wine 'foreign', 'outlandish'; *Elend* is the *Ausland* 'foreign country'. So the innkeeper would have done good business, at least up to 1914, by advertising, say, French wines as *elender* wine. We see a shift of meaning similar to the one in *Krank*.

The poet Geiler von Kaisersberg[4] speaks most peculiarly of a *hübschen* 'pretty' God. We couldn't say this today, but if you look it up in his works, you will find it more understandable. He meant with this a 'benevolent' God. *Hübsch* at that time carried the same shade of feeling as 'kind'. [An English example: when James II (1633-1701) first saw St. Paul's Cathedral in London, he called it *amusing, awful,* and *artificial.* He meant that it was 'pleasing to look at'; 'meriting awe'; and 'full of skilful artifice'.]

---

4. Geiler von Kaisersberg (1445–1510), famous preacher.

You will still find occasionally today surviving figures of speech, such as the phrase *ein ungehobelter Mensch* 'an uncouth person', literally 'unplaned' surface not smoothed with a *Hobel*, a carpenter's plane. You will understand this word on meeting it in Martin Luther's writing, that people are *gehobelt* 'planed smooth' by the prophets, that is, they are being put to rights, put in order, straightened up by the prophets. We find there the visual imagery of the act of planing with the 'making straight' in a moral sense.

After these examples from so far back in time, we can look at something closer to us. Lessing,[5] who lived more recently, wanted to describe the many things for which we rightfully develop great sympathy but which nevertheless cannot be called beautiful or be thought of as objects of art. By the way he phrased this, it can easily be misunderstood today: "Much of the *Anzüglichsten*, ('offensive, suggestive, lewd' in today's meaning) cannot be an object of art." [Modern German uses another form of the verb *anziehen*, 'to draw or pull': *anziehend* = 'attractive'.] Lessing means that many things of the most attractive nature cannot rightfully be called objects of art; in this word we have a real change on how the word is felt. We use the term nowadays for something essentially different.

It is interesting to trace the complicated way such shifts of meaning take place. Consider how the word *krank*, meaning 'slim' at an earlier time, might also be applied to a reed. A reed is *krank* when it is slim, less useful than a short, thick one. This shade of meaning gradually changed then to its present sense of 'sick', though somewhat modified once again. Adelung,[6] living halfway between that time and ours, speaks about *gekränkte*

---

5. Gotthold Ephraim Lessing (1729–1781), critic and dramatist. The quotation is from his play *Emilia Galotti*, Act I, Scene 4.
6. Johann Christoph Adelung, (1732–1806), German philologist and grammarian. Court librarian at Dresden.

ships that need repair [*gekränkte*, the past participle of the verb *kränken*, introduces still another shade of meaning. Today it is used to mean 'hurt', in the sense of hurt feelings.] It strikes us as a little comic or at least it characterizes the speaker as a joker when someone talks about a 'hurt clock', but in those years the sense of the word was perfectly clear, with its changed meaning, when applied to inorganic objects. *Krank* originally referred to the shape or form; the present meaning 'sick' crept in only gradually. While the earlier meaning 'slim' was cast aside altogether and the totally new one took over, we are still reminded of the original meaning by the term 'hurt ships'. The immediate sensing of the emotional, perceptive quality within words disappeared more and more.

Even Goethe still had a clear feeling about words; he found feelings in words that nowadays leave us cold, for in many respects he went back to the power of the language-forming genius. The word *bitter* 'bitter', for instance, has become for us a purely subjective tasting experience; usually we don't connect it in our feeling with what in earlier times was clearly visualized as *beissen* 'to bite', from which it originates. The relationship is there: whatever tastes *bitter* really 'bites us'. Goethe still felt this and writes about "*the bitter scissors of the Fates*"[7]—they are the *biting* scissors of the Fates! People nowadays are such abstract creatures that they think this is "mere poetic license." But it is not poetic license at all; it arose directly out of inner experience. True, Goethe did not yet live in a time when ninety-nine percent of poetic writing is superfluous. We should keep in mind while reading his work how within language he felt a much greater aliveness, a more inward life, than we are able to feel today as products of modern education. You can sense this, too, from Goethe's words, *Ein Ecce Homo gefiel mir wegen seiner*

---

7. In his poem "Harzreise im Winter" (Winter Journey in the Harz).

erbärmlichen Darstellung, 'An *Ecce Homo* painting pleased me particularly because of its miserable portrayal'. No one today seems to feel that there is anything more in Goethe's phrase than the meaning of a poor sort of representation. But Goethe wants to suggest that our deepest pity is aroused through this particular portrayal. We would say, *"Ein Ecce Homo gefiel mir wegen seiner Erbarmen heransfordernden Darstellung,"* 'An *Ecce Homo* painting pleased me particularly because the portrayal aroused compassion'. Goethe was still able to put it ' . . . because of its miserable portrayal'.

Not so very long ago it was possible to say of a person who liked to speak with children or poor people on the street, who was not snobbish or conceited, for whom one wished to show one's approval, *"Du bist ein niederträchtiger Mensch!"* Present meaning: 'You are a low-thinking person, low-minded, vile'. This was possible until the middle of the eighteenth century. *Ein niederträchtiger Mensch* was until that time an 'affable, amiable' person. He was being praised, given the highest praise from a certain point of view. Again, I do not believe that many people can still derive the right meaning from reading in eighteenth century literature about an *ungefährliche Zahl* a 'harmless number'; *ungefähr* now means 'approximate' not 'undangerous'. We would say today: 'a number that is approximately correct'. An *ungefährliche* number was simply an 'approximate' one.

Further, what would modern minds connect with the common eighteenth century expression, *unartige Pflaumen* 'naughty plums'. *Un* = 'not'; *Art* = 'type, sort, variety'. *Unartige* plums are those that do not show the specially typical marks of their kind, because they are an unusual variation.

Only when we acquire a feeling for the fact that such changes take place will we understand other changes that are not so obvious. For instance, our word *schwierig* 'difficult'—

you know the shade of feeling with which it is spoken. It was formerly used only with the conscious intention of expressing full of *Schwären*, full of *Geschwüre* 'swellings, abscesses'. Therefore if you found something *schwierig*, you wished to express the feeling that this would 'result in abscesses'. A very pictorial, vigorous expression to connect with our word *schwierig*.

Such things fall totally outside our modern nuances of feeling; they prove how wrong it is to judge language in a pedantic way without recognizing the reality of language metamorphosis, something also evident in dialects. Today, when offering a guest a meal with many courses, you might tell him not to eat too much of this or that because other dishes are coming for which he should save some appetite; you might say, "Please don't eat too much—there's a good dessert coming." But in one region of the German-speaking lands, it is possible to put it, "*Iss von dieser Speise nicht zuviel, es gibt noch etwas hintenauf*" 'Don't eat too much of this; there's still something coming in the rear'. [*Etwas hintenauf* in modern German carries the connotation that a 'spanking is in the offing'.]

In another dialect it is possible to say, "Oh, these are good children; *die schlachten sich*," 'they slaughter each other'. This meant that they take after their good parents, are cast in the same mold [*vom gleichen Schlag sein*]. It is exactly this kind of example that points up the living interchange between inner sensitivity and the external image in our feeling for language.

Sometimes this shows up in extremely important matters. For instance, you will find a statement of Goethe, made in his later years, characterizing his work on *Faust*. It has played a most significant role with the *Faust* commentators. In Goethe's last letter [March 17, 1832] addressed to Wilhelm von Humboldt, he characterized his work on *Faust* as remarkable *wenn seit über 60 Jahren die Konzeption des "Faust" bei ihm jugendlich von vorne herein klar, die ganze Reihenfolge hin weniger ausführlich vorlag*

(... when for more than sixty years the conception of *Faust* has been clear to me *from the beginning*, first as a young person; the whole sequence, however, less fully developed). Many *Faust* commentators concluded from this that Goethe already as a young man had a plan for the complete *Faust* that he had conceived clearly from the beginning (*von vorn herein*) and that the later work was merely a kind of working out the details. And much that is unnecessary and untrue in their characterization of his work on *Faust* has originated from this interpretation of the passage, for only since Fresenius [8] published his findings about the significance for Goethe of the phrase *von vorne herein* 'in from the front', that is, 'at the outset' has it been possible to understand Goethe's words. All this had special meaning for me because I worked with Fresenius [9]. When he had found something of importance, it often took decades before he did anything about it. Therefore I pressed him to publish this, for what he had to say was extremely important. You can put together all the passages of Goethe using the phrase *von vorne herein* and you will find that he never uses it in any but a spatial sense. If he said he had read a book *von vorne herein*, he meant that he had read only the beginning pages. It can be clearly shown that he had in his youth a clear conception of the first scenes of *Faust*. Here then simply a correct understanding of word usage explains Goethe's work; from this phrase you can see that what he could visualize spatially has for us become abstract. *Von vorne herein* he always used visually, spatially. Much of Goethe's charm and attraction for us is founded on his going back to the original qualities of the language-creating genius. You can start out from

---

8. August Fresenius (b. 1850). See Rudolf Steiner, *The Course of My Life* (Hudson, NY: Anthroposophic Press, 1951), pp. 221–223 .
9. From 1890 to 1897 in the Goethe-Schiller Archives in Weimar as editor of Goethe's *Scientific Writings*.

Goethe's language and from there search your way into Goethe's soul, instead of proceeding only materialistically as modern investigators do, and you will find there important criteria for freeing philology from rationalistic materialism. It is good to look for help from such sources also.

In many ways there no longer exists such language that expresses a combination of shades of feeling and sound. We can still find this sometimes in dialects, which also have it in themselves to bring the visual to expression. For instance, you will find here and there in dialect—more often than in educated speech—the phrase *unter den Arm greifen* 'to help someone'; literally 'to reach under his arm'. This simply means to come to the aid of a person who needs help. Why? Because a young person in offering a hand to someone elderly, who can't get about so easily any more, reaches under the other's arm to give support. This active image was transferred then to any helpful act. Exactly as it was with the expression (Lecture 2) "to wipe the *night-sleep* out of our eyes," so it is with the act of giving help, a single specific procedure chosen to express visually a more abstract generality. Sometimes the genius of language was no longer able to retain the visual element; then also from time to time imagery was retained in one instance, cast off in the other.

There still exists today the word *lauschen* 'listen with inner attentiveness' for a certain kind of listening. The Austrian dialect also has a word related to *lauschen*: *losen*. We not only say in Austria when we want to make a person listen, *Hör einmal* 'listen', but also *Los amol!* 'harken!'. *Losen* is a weaker but still active listening. Educated colloquial German has retained *lauschen*. *Losen* is a cognate with the feeling of a somewhat weak activity, even with a certain sneakiness, pointing to a secret kind of listening. In a sense *losen* has taken on the meaning of forbidden listening. For instance, when a person puts his ear to the keyhole or listens in when two are discussing something not meant for his hearing, then the word *losen* is used 'harken'.

Only after becoming sensitive to the feeling element in such sound sequences can one proceed to develop a sense for the basic sounds, the vowels and consonants. In the Austrian dialect there is a word *Ahnl* for grandmother. Do you perhaps know the word *Ahnl*? A more general term is *Ahnfrau* (*der Ahn, die Ahne*, male and female grandparents/progenitors). In *Ahnl* you have *Ahne* combined with an /l/. If you want to understand what is happening there in the realm of speech, you must swing up to a heightened feeling of /l/ as a consonant. Feel the /l/ in the suffix *-lich* ('-ly', as in *friendly*. See lecture 2 and lecture 4), in which I have explained that it originated from *leik*. It is somehow related to the feeling that something is moving about, that this moving about has to be imitated in the language. An *Ahnl* is a person who is clearly old but who makes the impression of being lively and mobile; you hardly notice the wrinkles in her face! You see the character of /l/ as it is used here.

Take the word *schwinden* 'dwindle, fade': to go away, to make a thing go away so that it can't be seen any more. Now figure that I don't really want to make it go away, but I want to cheat a little in seeming to make it go away. I want to effect something that is not a true, honest disappearance—but I would also feel a moving around, an /l/ as in the *Ahnl*—and there is the word *schwindeln* 'to swindle'. The /l/ makes the difference. You can feel exactly the subtly nuanced value of /l/ by going from *schwinden* to *schwindeln*. [Parallels in English would be *tramp-trample, side-sidle, tread-treadle*.]

If you dwell on these thoughts, eurythmy[10] will become completely natural. You will feel that eurythmy springs from

---

10. See Rudolf Steiner, *Eurythmy as Visible Speech*, GA 279, lecture 4 (New York: Anthroposophic Press, 1931).

our ancient, original relationship to the sound elements of words, which without the sound elements only movement can bring to expression. If you can feel such a thing, then you will be able to sense precisely how, for instance, in the vowel /u/ (*ooh*) there is an element of moving close together, snuggling close together. Look at how you do the /u/ in eurythmy [Arms and hands are brought close and parallel to each other, as in the written letter]. You have the moving together, the closeness of the gesture, so that you can say, in the word *Mutter* 'mother'—someone you usually come close to—it would be impossible to have an /a/ (ah) or /e/ (ay) as the strong vowel in the word. [The /o/ of 'mother' is a gesture of affection.] You can't imagine saying *Metter* or *Matter*. *Mater* shows that the language in which it occurs, Latin, was already a weakened one; the original word was *Mutter*.

I have shown you, with all this, the path of the genius of language, a path on which a barrier was erected, I have said, between the sound element of a word and its meaning. They were originally closely united with each other in subjective human perception. They have separated. The sound-content descends into the subconscious; the mental picture ascends into our consciousness [see lecture 4, page 59, 60]. Much has been cast off that can be perceived just there where human beings originally lived closely connected with the things and activities around them. When we go back to earlier times in language development, we find the altogether remarkable fact that the original forms of language take us completely out into factual reality, that there exists on the primitive levels of language formation a fine sense for actual facts, and that the people who live at this level live closely connected with things and with everything that goes on with things. The moment this living connection is broken, the sense for reality becomes hazy and people live in an unreality that expresses itself in abstract language.

In the original Indo-European language there were three genders, as in Latin. We still have three genders in German. You can feel three different qualities expressed as masculine, feminine, and neuter. In French there are only two genders left, in English only one. This shows us that the English language has divested itself with a grand gesture, one could say, of the sense for reality, that it now merely hovers over things but no longer lives in actualities. On that early step of human development when the gender of words was being formed, there still existed a primitive clairvoyance; a living, spiritual quality was perceived within things. *Der Sonne* 'sun', masculine and *die Mond* 'moon', feminine which later were reversed to *die Sonne* and *der Mond* [in modern German sun is feminine, moon is masculine] could never have come about in the older Indo-European languages had the elemental beings living in the sun and moon not been experienced as brothers and sisters. In antiquity the sun was felt to be the brother, the moon the sister. Today in German it has been turned around. The day was perceived as the son and the night as the daughter of the giant Norwi. This definitely originates from primitive clairvoyant vision. The feeling for the earth at that time was very different from the geologists' perception of it today, when they would actually have good reason to use the neuter gender and speak of *das Erde* [the correct form in modern German is *die Erde*, feminine]. People nowadays no longer sense that the earth in fact is Gaia, for whom the masculine god is Uranos. People still had a perception of this in the areas where the Germanic language was originally formed.

In any case there were shades of feeling arising out of the close connection with the world outside and these were the source for determining gender, for deciding characteristic gender. The elephant (*der Elefant*) was considered strong, the mouse (*die Maus*) weak. Since a man was perceived as strong and a woman weak, the elephant was given the masculine gender, the mouse the feminine. The trees of the forest are usually feminine because for the original perception, they were the dwelling places of female divinities. Of immense importance because it points to a deep aspect of the language genius is the fact that alongside the masculine and feminine genders there exists a neuter gender. We say *der Mann* 'the man', *die Frau* 'the woman', *das Kind* 'the child'. The child's gender or sex [the German language uses the same word *Geschlecht* for both] is not yet articulated, has not yet reached complete definition, is in the process of becoming. When the neuter gender arose, it came up out of a certain mood in the folk-genius, a feeling that anything given a neuter gender would only later become what it was to be. *Gold* does not yet have the special characteristic it will have someday. It is still young in the cosmos; it is not yet what it is destined to be. Hence it is not *der Gold* or *die Gold* but *das Gold*.

On the other hand we can look at what comes about when the visualizing power that could characterize gender disappears. We say today *die Mitgift* (dowry, literally 'with-gift'), which shows a clear connection to an earlier word *die Gift*. We also say today *der Abscheu* ('aversion', literally 'away-shyness') which is clear evidence of an earlier word *der Scheu*. Both these deductions are correct. *Der Scheu* and *die Gift* have gone through a subtle change in connotation. *Die Gift* in early times simply meant 'the noncommittal act of giving'. But because of what some people have given and what was, also in Faust's opinion, harmful to others, the word has changed its meaning and has been applied to gifts that are objectionable, losing the connection with the original gender characteristic. The result is *das Gift* 'poison', neuter gender. When a person once was called *scheu*, he was considered as having strong feelings, as being firm in himself. When the word became weak, it became *die Scheu* 'shyness', feminine.

That our language has become more abstract, that it has released itself from its interweaving with outer reality, can best be understood from the fact that the ancient Indo-European languages had eight cases: nominative, genitive, dative, accusative, vocative, ablative, locative, and instrumental [German has retained the first four. English has one case form for nouns, except for possessives—usually adding /s/—and two forms *you*, *your* or three forms *they, them, their* for pronouns]. This means that not only was the position of a thing expressed as it is done today with the first four cases, but people were also able to follow other relationships with their feelings. For instance, to do a thing at a certain time, we can express as *diesen Tag* 'on this day', accusative, or *dieses Tages* 'of this day', genitive. No longer do we experience the active helpfulness of the day, of the time of day, or of a special day in particular. No longer do we have the experience that whatever is done on the second of January, 1920, for instance, could not be accomplished later, that time is a helpful element, that time is involved in something that helps us. There existed a sense for all this in earlier ages when the instrumental case was used, *hiu tagu*. We would have to say something like *durch diesen Tag* 'through this day', *vermittelst dieses Tages* 'by means of this day'. *Hiu tagu* has become the word *heute* 'today'; the old instrumental case is buried in the word, just as *hiu jaru* has become *heuer* 'this year'. But German has retained only four cases and cast off the others. You will understand from this how continuously language becomes more and more abstract, and how the capacity for abstract thought with its definite lack of a sense for reality has been taking the place of an earlier connection with the real world. This is what language reveals.

The Inner Path
of the Genius of Language

I HAVE shown you a few characteristic examples of language development and believe that now you should be able to visualize the inner journeying of the language-forming genius. If you hope to find your way through the phenomena of language and its evolution, you will have to understand the guidelines such phenomena reveal. Of course, I have been able to show you only a few things; today I will point out only one important guideline, summarizing these basic thoughts. I hope we will be able very soon to continue this study.[1] Certainly the main thing you will have understood is how the human beings in a primitive stage of language development were receptive, inwardly alive, to the consonance of sound and object. Whether this object is an inner feeling, an external event, an external thing, or an external fact doesn't matter. Whenever it is essential to form sounds that will express inner feelings or perceptions about whatever is outside us, then the sounds will be of vowel quality in the broadest sense. Vowel character in language denotes everything formed inwardly,

---

1. While it never came to another course on language, there is much material given by Rudolf Steiner from 1920 to 1924 in the *Conferences with the Teachers of the Waldorf School in Stuttgart* (4 Vols). See also page 131.

everything that is being felt inwardly and that presses itself into the sound out of what we are experiencing in our feeling and will. Hence we will find in all the *vowels* and *vowel forms* the feelings and will-impulses that are called forth in us by the outer world and in a way are thrust into our larynx. In everything to do with consonants we will find gestures modeled on what we perceive in the outer world.

Let us suppose we would like to speak about an angle. First, we have an image of a certain angle in mind. To describe the sides of the angle with our hand, we would do this [Rudolf Steiner makes a gesture]. What we do like this with our hand, we actually do with our organs of speech in forming certain consonants. Language is in this respect only the audible expression of gestures that are not being made externally with the limbs but with much finer parts of the human organism, our beneficent air-organism. If you think about these inner laws, you will gradually develop the insight that language imitates either the outer world directly or imitates what we experience in the outer world through our feelings and sense perceptions.

Let us imagine ourselves facing two possibilities: We could do either one thing or the other. Instinctively we begin to turn over in our thoughts whether we should do this or that. If we are still more or less an "imitating animal," as of course everyone is on a primitive level of language development, relationship to the outer world still transmits itself into an external gesture; we do this [gesture to the right and to the left]. We have to decide between our right side and our left side. That is, we are expressing the phenomenon that internally we are split in two, because two different, external facts are confronting us. We split ourselves into two parts in order to determine toward which side the stronger weight in our thinking tends. So we do this [repeats the gesture]. We separate, we decide, and also divide. But of course, if we are to come to a favorable decision we have to go back to the past as far as possible. Hence we not only divide ourselves (*teilen*, 'to divide') but we divide ourselves far back to the beginning (*ur-teilen*); we make an archetypal, original division. [See Lecture 4, page 52,53.] The word *Urteil* 'judgment' should definitely be understood as a gesture transformed inwardly into sound. All consonant-forming is gesture-forming that has simply been transformed into speech sounds.

When we search for the basis of this metamorphosis, we can trace it throughout the whole course of language development. At first human beings lived more fully outside themselves in their surroundings. Only gradually did they become inward beings. To begin with, they lived in the outer world, closely connected to the things around them, especially in the very ancient times when an original, primitive clairvoyance still existed. At this time human beings thought very little about themselves nor did they have any definite ideas about themselves. They knew, however, that there were all sorts of ghosts, all kinds of elemental spirits, which they perceived in what we now call external objects. Even in himself a person still saw an elemental being. "You," he said to himself, "have come through your father and mother into this world." He objectified himself. We find that on the first level of language-formation the language-forming genius, to begin with, brings about mainly consonant sounds. The primitive languages on the whole must have had consonantal character, because the primitive peoples were still without inwardness. Primitive peoples today, at least the ones who have remained at this original level, have rich consonant formations in their language; the consonant sounds show clearly the imitation of external events: for instance, *Schnalzer* ['tongue-clickers', both words good examples of an accumulation of consonants. Laurens van der Post, in *The Lost World of the Kalahari*, has described the Bushman's language: "the sound of natural relish that the word *ghwai Xkhwe* makes

on his lips is a joy to hear, and the click of the complex consonants flashes on his tongue as he utters them like a sparkle of
sun on a burst of flower from our somber mountain gorse."].
Certain African tribes are able to use the human organs of
speech to produce sounds like the sharp snapping of a whip.
'Tongue clicking' disappears when human beings begin to
express more of their inner feelings through sound structure.
Consonant formations must be considered the first step. Then
the second step will be the vowel formations, but the inwardness found in vowel formations is actually a stage of transition.
Finally signs of aging in the genius of language appear: the
vowel-forming power recedes and the consonant-forming
power comes to the fore again.

Our human language journey involving the development of
language proceeds essentially from outward to inward and then
from inward to outward. We can observe this procedure
directly in the sound-structure; it is the intrinsic essential fact
throughout the whole forming of language. It is the intrinsic,
essential fact to such a degree that we encounter it in every
aspect of language. That first step of language development we
meet everywhere: human beings, still selfless, unaware of themselves, create language. We are continually impelled to bring a
word designating one thing towards another word in an external manner [as in early English: *sea-horse,* meaning 'ship']. On
this level, human beings are altogether very lively in themselves. Later, when they become more inward and spiritual, a
bit of this primitive liveliness is lost to them. They become
more enclosed, more rigid, more abstract, and no longer have
the strength to pour into the word itself what they see externally; instead, they add onto it [that is, using combining forms:
prefixes and suffixes].

To study such phenomena, we should find the following
characteristic examples exceedingly interesting. There is, for

instance, in Old High German the verb *salbom*, in modern German *ich salbe* 'I am anointing'; cognate, *salve*). You can take this through first, second, and third person:

salbom, 'I anoint'	salbomes, 'we anoint'
salbos, 'you anoint'	salbot, 'you anoint' (pl)
salbot, 'he' or 'she anoints'	salbont, 'they anoint'

In these six words conjugating the verb 'to anoint', you always have *salbo* as the verb proper, denoting the activity. What is added creates the designated person of the word, for *I* the *m*, for *you* in the singular the *s*, for *he* or *she* the *t*, for *we* the *mes*, for *you* in the plural the *t*, for *they* the *nt*. The fact that these suffixal forms are still contained within the verb is understandable in the following sense: The contrasts of '*I, you, he, we, you, they*' appear at this primitive step because human beings looked at them very much from the outside. They added the person-sounds directly to the sounds that express activity. They were still inwardly lively enough to connect the person-sounds in a living way with the verbal form for the action. We should consider this twofoldness: first, the early attention directed toward the outer world, and second, the addition of the main word itself to the inward, lively, transformative force. This '*I, you, he, she, it*' was not originally felt to be an organic part of the verb or to be something of inwardness. You can observe this in the related Sanskrit language where the person-designation is simply stuck onto the most important word; it is to be found as an independent designation for '*I, you, he, she, it*'. The '*m*' in Old High German is simply the metamorphosis *of mi* 'I' of Sanskrit; the *s*, the metamorphosis of *si* 'you', singular, of Sanskrit; *t*, the *ti* 'he, she, it'; *mes*, the *masi* 'we'; *t*, the transformed *tasi* ('you', plural); *nt* is the suffix

-anti 'they', spoken somewhat hastily. You can still observe in Sanskrit that it is not at all a question of conjugating the central part of the main verb and then perceiving the change of form as a designation of person. No, at that time human beings were inwardly so alive that with their perception of the outer world, they were able to organize the grammar of personal pronouns into a sound-sequence expressing the main idea. That is an important difference. You might easily believe that at this primitive level there would be mainly an inward modulating of words. No, there is not. An inner aliveness in the people lets them connect the two components of a word together. This is a consonantal activity, not a vowel-forming one.

When later a language like Latin reaches the next level, with the perception that the personal pronouns should be within the inner organism of the sound sequence, the language has arrived at a level corresponding to a greater inwardness of that particular language genius. Toward inwardness it has worked its way from outwardness where it has simply attached to the end of a word what it perceived as an external element: *salbom*, 'I anoint', *salbos*, 'you anoint'. Just as on a primitive level people don't say *Karl Meyer* but the *Meyer-Karl* [peasant dialect], so it is with such verbs; whatever makes them specific is added at the end. Here, too, the specific pronoun is put at the end of the word.

Repositioning the pronoun from the end of the word to the beginning and making it an independent word was the path to the greatest inwardness, the kind of inwardness that perceives how spiritually abstract our inner nature really is. Now the person is separated off and placed ahead of the verb. You can learn something important from this procedure if you go back to the primitive constructions of the language-forming genius that does not really know anything about an *I* or a *you* separated from external things, and that still presses into the word whatever has to be said about *I* or *you*. Later, the genius finds the pronouns within the word itself—Latin is a language at this level—and plucks them out, comes to a mirror image of itself, comes to ego consciousness, and then puts the *I* and the *you* up ahead of the verb. This growing sense of egoism, this arrival at self-visualization is reflected quite clearly in language development. One can say that becoming aware of oneself at a certain unconscious level has been achieved as the result of the ancient Apollonian precept "know thou thyself"; this was followed everywhere in the languages of the western world by taking the personal pronouns out of the verb forms. These forms could still express human inwardness; they had not yet separated themselves completely away from it. You really will not be able to study languages unless you do what I suggested yesterday: consider them as the expression of human soul development.

You see, from language that is still alive it is quite possible to trace the "remnants" of the vowel-forming and consonant-forming powers. There is a quality in the verbs, the words of action, that gives them a vowel-forming character and makes the vowel in them the main element. With a little reflection you will realize that the verbs in which the vowel element—expressing inner sensitivity—is more important than the consonants are those that describe an activity we can connect ourselves with inwardly and wholeheartedly.

Now observe that there is a difference between the state of your soul right now and how it was a little while ago. You are sitting here and you have been sitting quite a while. Whatever is expressed by this sitting is something you have connected yourself with; it is connected quite inwardly with you. You have come to sit here by setting yourself down. With the setting yourself down you are connected much less inwardly; it is more external. You can't continue to 'set' yourself down for any length of time because you can't connect yourself so closely with the act of dropping onto a chair, but you can sit for half an hour and even longer, because it is possible to connect yourself inwardly with sitting. It is really the case that you should experience the sound-sequence for *sitting* as vowel-articulated, and the one for *setting* as more external, more consonantal. If you are sensitive to vowel articulation, you will have the power—through the language-forming genius—to be creative with vowels; you will do this by adapting the word in various ways: *sit, sat, sat* [the German *sitzen, sass, gesessen* has one additional vowel change]. With the consonantal activity, expressed in *setting*, you keep the emphasis on the consonants instead of forming a vowel change to *satting* or something similar [the German *setzen, setzte, gesetzt*, 'to set', has no vowel change]. You are depicting something external with this by saying *set*. If you want to express the fact that this took place some time ago, you will say *set-did* (*setzen tat*). [The English verb *to set* is irregular and does not follow the German rule. We have substituted the verb *to place* in this discussion.] You will say *place-did*. You do place yourself, you did place yourself; in metamorphosis this becomes *placed*, for the *-ed* is the transformed *did*.

People who still today have kept something of this language-forming strength in themselves will emphasize consonants just as happened in earlier times. If they belong to a more primitive level of culture, they have an unusual capacity to imitate outer life and activity with their consonantal sound-structures, using as few vowels as possible. You can hear something of this joining together of sound and outer action in the words of a somewhat simple peasant who had considered it an honor to have his son study at the university. He was asked what his son was doing at the university. For the time being, the son was using his inheritance not so much for steeping himself in the abstract and mental side of academic life but rather for giving himself over to more external aspects. And so the father, when asked what his son was doing, said, "Strolling around he does, loafing around he does, beer guzzling he does, whooping it up he does, but doing something he doesn't do (*aber tun tut er nichts!*)."

A strong feeling of inwardness streams into the language-forming verb. In the sound structures that have retained their character, especially their conceptual character, you will always come to feel that the vowel change in verbal conjugations (an *ablaut*, as 'come, came') expresses something we are more inwardly connected with. On the other hand, we will not be able to develop the ablaut with verbs for which we have an inner mental image but with which we cannot connect ourselves inwardly, verbs that do not become something we feel but remain something merely observed. When you say, *I sing, I sang*, you have the ablaut. It is quite different when you say, *I singe*, 'I burn something'. The word *singe* has its sound structure because fire *sings*. *I singe* = *I am* making something 'sing'. If you are singing, you are connecting yourself inwardly with what you want to express through the sound-sequence. If you singe, you are not connecting yourself with it inwardly; you are looking at it by looking at yourself from outside—hence there is no vowel change: *I singe, I singed* [the corresponding words in German are *singen*, 'sing', and *sengen*, 'singe']. Whenever we fail to notice such things today it is because the words have changed so strongly that nothing of the kind is evident. We have to go back then to earlier forms of the sound structure. It is extremely important for us to follow these three steps: the connection of our life first with the outer world, then with growing inwardness, and finally the next step of inwardness where a human being explains his or her own inner world with words such as the personal pronouns. You will come to understand language formation much more easily for yourself if you follow this process. It seems that language is a flowing together of the thought element and the will element in the human being; it appears that on its first primitive level wherever the speech sound is still strongly connected with the mental image, it is even difficult to distinguish the thought element from the will element. Today our speaking, particularly in Modern German, is already bound to our will to an extraordinary degree. In German we speak with our will and learn to use our will as a matter of course when we learn to speak. We also accompany our speech with the ideas and images we have become used to bringing together with expressions of will.

It is totally different in English. For someone who is impartial and can observe such things, it is an entirely different human activity to speak German than it is to speak English, though low German dialects have remained closer to English. In speaking English it is much more the case that thinking goes into the speaking, that is, into the development of the sounds. In German, thinking does not take place in the unfolding of the sounds but proceeds as a parallel phenomenon to the sound development. In general, the western languages have preserved themselves much more from this instinctive bringing together of sound and mental image than have the Central European languages. Therefore, the western European languages have taken on such a rigid structure. In them hardly anything can be formulated without someone saying, "You can't say it like that, you have to change it around." This doesn't happen in German, where it's possible to say it in almost any way. You can put the subject anywhere, at the beginning or at the end, for the thought goes somewhat separately from the sound-structure, parallel with it, further removed than in the Western languages. Only by turning back to the earlier stages of our German language development do we arrive at an increasingly strict connection between mental image and sound. Therefore the quality still present in the western languages is an atavistic throwback that can be studied by means of the earlier steps in German and in our dialects.

If you feel your way vividly into language from this point of view, you will be led at the same time into the essential nature of the folk souls. Suppose you are looking at an object in front of you. As primitive people we have formed a sound sequence for this object out of consonant and vowel elements. So we say *Wagen* ['wagon', 'car'; Anglo-Saxon, *wain*] for something that can be put in motion. If we have in front of us the same object in the plural, that is, a number of such objects, we form the plural by saying *die Wägen*, by forming the 'Umlaut'. It is true, *die Wagen* is also correct, but it belongs to literary language and was not really formed within the organism of the language. [The difference of pronunciation in English would be parallel to the vowels of *far* and *vague*.]

Why do we form the umlaut? It was for the singular object that we put the sounds together, and in doing so our consciousness was sparked, lit up, enlivened; at that moment we were awake and attentive. When we formed the plural, we had less overview and therefore had the need to express it in a more nebulous way. We dimmed the pure /a:/ sound [as in 'ah'] to a murky /e:/ (as in c<u>a</u>re). The original sound sequence is always formed by consciously observing the actual facts or sensations. Whatever attracts less attention or cannot be closely observed reveals itself as dulled.[2] The important thing here is to see how something changes within the human being. The dialect of many German areas does not say *der Wagen* but *der Wogn*. Since the normal attention to sound sequence brought about an answering /o/, the dimming in the plural is expressed by *die Woagen*. You can follow this in many examples.[3]

---

2. See Rudolf Steiner, *Eurythmy as Visible Speech*, GA 279, lecture 7 (London: Rudolf Steiner Press, 1984).

One more thing I should like to call to your attention. As you know, lively mental images were the source of the consonantal forming of language in earlier times, and much of what was felt in the soul of ancient peoples flowed into this language forming; it can still be studied in what has been retained in primitive minds and feelings today. These perceptions, filled with an immense vitality at that time, were not only alive to the outer world through the senses but were also completely bound up with a kind of primitive clairvoyance. Otherwise there would not be all our sturdy, image-filled words that are happily still in existence. Here is an example: A person still living within the sphere of atavistic clairvoyance—no matter how weak—and possessing the ancient kind of perception was certainly able to perceive that the physical body of an ordinary human being contained something we call today the etheric body. Such a primitive person perceived the head [this and the following were illustrated on the blackboard] and, projecting beyond it, a second, etheric head. He felt that the head was the expression of thinking. Thus we can say that primitive human beings with their original clairvoyance named the human being from the standpoint of thinking—with a word very much related to ours—by the word *Manas*, for *Mensch* 'human being, Man, person'. *Mensch* is the same as *manas*, of course, this is the human being we usually come across. But that early, atavistically clairvoyant person knew that it's also possible to encounter other, somewhat different, people—here I'm joking about something one ought not to

---

3. Old English had many ways of forming noun plurals. The most common was the addition of *-an*, but *-as* (later *-es*, *-s*) gained ground and finally carried the day. However, we still have *oxen, children, kine, brethren*. The *mutation* plural (changing the vowel) we find in *geese, feet, mice, lice, men,* and *women*. None of these are changes to a dipthong, as in German.

make too trivial—who do not have the supersensible 'person' closely connected to the physical person so snugly and prosaically. In cases where the supersensible does not quite fit into the rest of the human being, people felt: the etheric body is *verrückt* ['shifted', literally 'moved off its place', a word that means today 'deranged', 'insane', 'crazy']. This was then transferred to the whole person: *Der Mensch ist verrückt* 'that person is shifted', i.e., 'crazy'. A purely external fact is described, the displacing of the etheric body. Just this sort of picture-making, going back to the time when pictures of the spiritual world could still be observed, is exceedingly interesting. If people would only recognize this, if learned philologists were not so sound asleep, proceeding as they do quite superficially on their materialistic tracks! If they would enter instead into the inward soul element that finds its expression in external language-forming, philology would turn of itself into a science of the soul and then into spiritual science. For this reason it is a shame that philology has become so materialistic; young people actually have no opportunity to observe the effects of soul and spirit on the forming of language.

I believe that in some way now what I've wanted to give you in the way of guidelines and examples can be useful to those of you who are teachers at the Waldorf School. Take them into your mind and soul; they will serve as a stimulus to observe the many elements of language that you can make use of in your teaching. If you have taken into yourself the spirit of looking at things in this way, it will definitely benefit your classes; speech will always be the connecting link between you and your students. It would be of enormous help to try on your own to bring back into words some of the original strength of feeling and image-making in language. Through this you will train yourself to a more lively perception than one otherwise is able to develop. Actually we modern people walk around much like living corpses, largely because our language has plunged so drastically out of our hearts and has fallen down somewhere below. It has become an unconscious element of will. We can no longer feel how our soul qualities are alive within the spoken /e/ and /u/ and /a/ and /m/. We no longer train ourselves to imbue the words that sound alike with the very same inward feelings. We are abstract not only in our understanding, in our thinking, but abstract also in our speaking. For a person who really has a lively feeling for language, much of what we speak today sounds like a record on a record-player, but the record had already been produced in ancient times. We must try to make a connection with our language again. However, for this a kind of self-education will be necessary, so that we learn to listen inwardly.

Let us listen to the word *rauh* 'rough' and feel the sound combination inwardly. If we say on perceiving this figure [a four-sided figure is drawn on the board], "That is a *Raute* 'rhomboid'," then we can sense *rough* in such a way that we feel roughness in the perception of the corners. We can still make the effort today, when looking at such a figure, to experience the corners as related to *rough*, and the /t/ of *Raute* we will feel as *tut* 'does'. Whatever *does rough* is the *Raute*. [We can approach this from many sides in English: even–evening; try–trisangle; hole–hold; flow–flower, etc.] Developing such imponderables would be an element of strength in teaching, if we tried not to allow sound-structure and mental image to diverge. I beg you to consider just what kind of a subtle background can we possibly sense when we talk to a child about this geometrical figure and say only, "This is a rhomboid"? We ourselves don't feel anything if we simply say, "This is a rhomboid." How strong a foundation we could establish for the attentiveness of the students that we need in our class if we will re-educate ourselves through an understanding of the sounds of speech, and then feel the need to educate our children in the same direction!

You can gain ideas for your self-education from just this view of language I have been talking about. But I've also wanted to show you something of method, my dear friends. My aim has been to guide you toward important ideas by means of characteristic, concrete examples. I believe that a truly modern university professor would probably expound in three volumes what I have developed in this short time. He would of course try for completeness, but it would be less possible for him to develop the guidelines to stimulate our thinking, our mental pictures, and our perceptions. If you proceed in the elementary school as we have proceeded in this language course, you will evolve a good basic method of your own. You will try at every point to look for thoroughly characteristic examples for what you are going to present to your students, and you will be able to combine what you see and feel in these characteristic examples with the perception of their spiritual quality.

There is truly no better method of pushing children into materialism than by giving them abstract instruction. A spiritual way of teaching is through concrete examples, but you must not forget to allow qualities of soul and spirit to reveal themselves in these very concrete examples. Therefore I believe that what I have given you in this course can be a practical, methodological extension of the course I gave before the Waldorf School began.[4] And I believe that you can accomplish a great deal by pondering, "How should I organize my class teaching, translating all this into what is right for children—for it is possible to adapt it in every subject—so that it follows this

4. See Rudolf Steiner, *The Study of Man* (London: Rudolf Steiner Press, 1975); *Practical Advice to Teachers* (London: Rudolf Steiner Press, 1976); *Discussions with Teachers* (Bristol, England: Rudolf Steiner Press, 1992).

process of drawing in a spiritual quality by means of concrete examples?" If you do this, you will not easily run the risk almost all teaching does of not getting finished with the load of subject matter. It is only when subject matter is shredded into atoms and systematized that you don't get finished with it, because it is so tempting to take up the single, atomized parts that are uncharacteristic and pile them up, trying to show what is characteristic. Of course, there are uncharacteristic examples in all the school subjects; using these means that a great deal has to be strung together. If you make the effort, however, to choose characteristic examples and develop what is spiritual through your examples, you will achieve a certain necessary economy in your teaching.

I would be happy, my dear friends—and let it be said in all friendship, especially to those who are teachers here at the Waldorf School—I would be happy if two things have been noted in these improvised talks: First, the stimulus toward educating yourselves in a kind of brotherly-sisterly alliance with the language genius; on the other hand, that the method of teaching is influenced to some extent by what I have just pointed out to you.

It is to be hoped that when I come back, possibly very soon, we will continue this exploration into language.

Rudolf Steiner on Language:
A View from Modern Linguistics

I

THE SPIRIT OF RUDOLF STEINER'S VIEWS ON LANGUAGE
VERSUS THE GHOST OF MODERN LINGUISTICS

The present book will be understandable in a general way to readers familiar with anthroposophy. They will read it as an extension of what they know of anthroposophy, the folk soul, and certain principles of Waldorf education. Such readers may be suspicious of the technical remarks that I, a linguist-anthroposophist, must make to bring anthroposophy into an equilibrium with linguistics. I can promise, however, that whatever footnotes or minor corrections I may have to add to Steiner's thought these do not detract in any way from the value of his insights. At the same time, of course, general readers, interested either in language or Waldorf education, should easily be able to find their own way through the shoals of these two somewhat specialized fields on the basis of common sense.

To someone familiar with the field of linguistics and unfamiliar with anthroposophy, on the other hand, some of Rudolf Steiner's remarks may ring as strange half-truths. An historical linguist will be impressed with Steiner's awareness of phonetic change, Grimm's Law, and most of the accurate and very interesting etymologies he brings out, particularly in Lecture 5. (Though there may be some raising of scholarly eyebrows at a few of the possibly false etymologies.) But the non-anthroposo-phist linguist will not know what to make of concepts like that of the folk soul, the ether body, the "Genius of Language," or the underlying assumption of "thinking-feeling-willing" and the idea that the written word is dead in comparison to spoken language.

Generally, modern, scientific linguists dismiss the Bible as a reliable source of information and pay little, if any, attention either to the Creative Word of God in Genesis or to the task of Adam in the Garden of Eden of giving every creature a name. They view the story of the Tower of Babel as a quaint, old-fash-ioned allegory to explain why there are about 5,000 languages on Planet Earth, and tend to associate the story of Pentecost and the Apostles' ability to "speak in tongues" either with med-ical hysteria or with modern people experiencing glossolalia when in a trance under mass hypnosis or some drug.

Yet modern linguists would not be unanimous in their bewilderment upon reading Steiner and some may feel more upset (or threatened) by some of Steiner's statements than by others. In fact, many linguists are showing signs of becoming tired of treating language as an abstract algebra—which has been the prevailing mode in the USA since 1957—and are willing at least to admit that there is such a thing as poetry. Some linguists even write good poems, but when asked how they achieved what they did, they cannot give an answer conso-nant with their beliefs about their discipline. They would prob-ably say that their writing ability is a special sort of "performance" or some unconscious talent they accidentally developed.

Why do we have this glaring gap? Is there a way to bridge it?

To lay the ground for answers to these questions, I shall briefly characterize modern linguistics for the general reader unfamiliar with modern, academic linguistics.

The field of linguistics has become extremely technical during the second half of the twentieth century. Many major statements in the field, such as Edward Sapir's *Language* and Leonard Bloomfield's similarly entitled book, appeared in America only after Rudolf Steiner's death in 1925. The dominant philosophy behind such language analysis was behaviorism, a mode of thinking imported from Russia, where Ivan Pavlov worked with the conditioned reflexes of dogs.[1] The stronghold of this movement in the USA was Johns Hopkins University; Yale and other leading schools followed it.

The development of the field of linguistics took an even further, more drastic turn after 1957, when work on Transformational-Generative Grammar was begun at the Massachusetts Institute of Technology.[2]

Transformational-Generative Grammar [or TGG as it is called] deserves a brief characterization here as it is the prevailing mode of doing linguistics, not only in America but in other countries as well.

The basic idea of TGG is that underlying all sentences in all languages is an abstract calculus or propositional logic—known as "deep structure"—from which various languages, by using various "transformations," create actual sentences. These real sentences are called "surface structures." How words are pronounced is a secondary matter. Chomsky, the inventor of TGG, considers phonology "interpretive." Actual meaning, too, used to be considered "interpretive" in TGG—what mattered more than anything else was the abstract, set-theory base,

---

1. See Edward Sapir, *Language* (New York: Harcourt Brace and World, 1926); and Leonard Bloomfield, *Language* (New York: Henry Holt & Co., 1933).
2. See Noam A. Chomsky, *Syntactic Structures* (The Hague: Mouton, 1957); also Noam A. Chomsky, *Aspects of the Theory of Syntax* (Cambridge, MA.: MIT Press, 1965).

and heavily math-like "deep structure" of the sentences, the so-called "deep syntax." Such a theory cannot account, for instance, for a speaker's tone of voice—whether what was said was said in jest or seriously. Facial gestures and hand motions are considered irrelevant: they belong to "performance." The real essence, according to the TGG view of language, is "deep syntax"—everything must be written. And yet sentences are viewed in isolation and not in paragraphs or chapters. They are not seen as the steps in an unfolding story.

Linguists embraced TGG for two reasons. First, because it was "explicit," and second, because Chomsky's political attitude appealed to them during the War in Vietnam.

TGG is very far removed from the anthroposophical view of language and makes sense only to those who, after a year of introductory courses in a graduate school, devote their attention to Transformational-Generative Grammar and its various offshoots.

I have always considered it most removed from actual reality and have been arguing against it throughout my professional career as a linguist. Reducing language to math-like logical propositions amounts to a lifeless, abstract atomization of meaning and must be seen as a result of the age of computerization that we inhabit. Nor is it the best way to computerize language, as Chomsky used the early IBM models of the late 'fifties and the 'sixties at MIT.

These two American developments—Bloomfieldian, behaviorist Structuralism and Chomsky-style Transformational-Generative Grammar—have been paralleled by a number of international developments, some of them actually a bit earlier than Chomsky, some coeval, and some subsequent to its appearance.

In the United States, there is Tagmemics, a brand of linguistics actually antedating Chomsky and practiced by Protestant missionaries.[3] Stratificational Grammar, invented by Sydney M. Lamb, who united the philosophy of the Danish scholar Louis Hjelmslev with American structuralism, also deserves mention.[4]

In the British Commonwealth, linguistics had been and continues to be practiced along different lines. Following the lead of J.R. Firth, the main mover of linguistics in the Commonwealth has been Michael A.K. Halliday.[5]

A powerful brand of Soviet mathematical linguistics grew up in Moscow under the leadership of Sebastian K. Shaumyan, who moved to the United States in 1975 and taught at Yale University for ten years before his retirement.[6]

The field, then, is quite vast and complex—comparing it to modern medicine, replete with general practitioners, pediatricians, ophthalmologists, podiatrists, gynecologists and psychiatrists, is not too great an exaggeration. None of this widely spread international scholarship, offering Ph.D. and M.A. degrees all over the United States and most other parts of the civilized world, existed at the time Steiner gave his six lectures on language to the assembled Waldorf teachers in Stuttgart—although Indo-European studies were already a

---

3. See Kenneth L. Pike, *Language in Relation to a Unified Theory of the Structure of Human Behavior* (The Hague: Mouton, 1967); and subsequent works by members of the Dallas-based Summer Institute of Linguistics [SIL].

4. See Louis Hjelmslev, *Prolegomena to a Theory of Language,* Franis J. Whitfield trans. (Madison: University of Wisconsin Press, 1943). Also see Sydney M. Lamb, *Outline of Stratificational Grammar* (Washington, D.C.: Georgetown University Press, 1966); and *Readings in Stratificational Grammar* (Adam Makkai & David G. Lockwood, eds., University of Alabama Press, 1973).

5. Perhaps the most characteristic of his many books are *Language as Social Semiotic* (London: Edward Arnold, 1978) and *Introduction to Functional Grammar* (London: Edward Arnold, 1985).

6. See his book *A Semiotic Theory of Language* (Bloomington, IN., Indiana University Press, 1987).

well established discipline practiced primarily in Germany, France and Great Britain.

We must also bear in mind that Steiner's own formal education was not in the field of linguistics. When he spoke about language, then, he did so both out of his general education—which was exceptionally wide and rich and covered ancient history, world literature, world philosophy—and his own personal spiritual investigations. Unfortunately, the latter are not yet the kind of research avenue with whose results one can easily come out and confront the international academic establishment.

It is unarguable, however, that Steiner correctly identified language as that area of human consciousness which, if properly understood and studied without the prejudices of the prevailing materialistic *Weltanschauung,* can lead to extremely valuable insights into the essential nature of human beings.

Steiner viewed language as the expression of our THINKING, FEELING, and WILLING, the familiar trichotomy that runs through the entire edifice of anthroposophical thought. It was inconceivable to Rudolf Steiner to view language as an arbitrary convention of consciously created symbols. Steiner was after something quite different. He sought the spiritual capacity of human beings to use their thinking, feeling, and willing through their voices to transmit contents of consciousness and to use their words as live entities that can eventually elevate us to the status of being co-creators with the spiritual world.

I think it must be obvious at this point that the "science of linguistics" as we know it today, cannot even approximate these goals.

Linguistics, in its various modes, is nevertheless one of the most important disciplines that human beings have developed throughout the course of evolution because—as I will suggest in the concluding section of this afterword—it is the prototypical consciousness soul discipline for our time which, if it is properly cultivated, will lead us to the ability to "think about thinking," which is a spiritual activity of consciousness in freedom.[7]

I will now turn to the various aspects of language that Steiner mentions in his six lectures, in a somewhat topical order.

II.

PHONETIC CHANGE AND
THE ETYMOLOGICAL MERRY-GO-ROUND

Nothing can be more telling about Rudolf Steiner's depth of insight into widely disparate subjects, than the number of *trouvailles* or "hits" he achieves in what is—admittedly—a merely improvised series of hastily arranged lectures at the request of a number of friends. Few, if any, during the course of the past two thousand years were able to do what Steiner did, day in and day out, during the entire course of his life.

Language was no exception in this regard. Steiner's intuitions, as seen from the vantage point of what we today consider

---

7. For "Consciousness soul" (*Bewusstseinseele*), see Rudolf Steiner, *Theosophy*, Chapter 1. Steiner describes there how the physical body is built up out of physical substances to meet the requirements of the thinking I. To this end, the physical body is permeated by life forces, which constitute a "life body" or "body of formative forces." As such, the living body opens to the senses, becoming a "soul body." As "sentient soul," it is open both to impressions from the outer world and to thinking. Through this, it becomes "mind" soul. And when this "mind soul" opens to intuitions from above (as well as sensations from below), it becomes the "consciousness soul, the "soul within the soul."The "age of the consciousness soul"—when the I becomes active in humanity—is Rudolf Steiner's designation for the evolutionary state of consciousness entered by humanity around the end of the fifteenth century. Georg Kühlewind (see note 21) has suggested that the three prototypical consciousness soul disciplines are linguistics, psychology, and epistemology.

scientific linguistics were all on the right track, even if the scientific research of one hundred years has come up with some details that a non-specialist could not have been aware of in the nineteen twenties.

One of the purposes of this Afterword is to indicate both the limitations of scientific linguistics and some of the inevitable gaps in the technical knowledge of this field in anthroposophical literature in order that the outlines of a future synthesis may be attempted in a concluding section. Today we know for certain that a language cannot possibly be just a huge collection of data, whether stored on the magnetic tape of some recording device or transcribed by hand using the International Phonetic Alphabet—the IPA. We know that defining language as it was defined in the late forties by Bernard Bloch and George L. Trager, while working sufficiently well for the field anthropologist after World War II in exotic places, is no longer really tenable in 1994.[8] Bloch and Trager wrote: "A language is an arbitrary set of vocal noises by means of which members of a speech community interact." Generations of structuralists were brought up with this definition of language, and people seldom challenged it.

It is immediately noticeable that this definition is couched in terms of behaviorist psychology and that, as such, it is a materialistic view of humankind's most precious possession, language.

Whereas it is true that we all make "vocal noises" when we speak, language consists of far more than just speech sounds. We have five thousand years of world literature to back up this claim: writing is an essential part of language. So is hand signing by the deaf and the use of Braille by the blind. Without gestures

---

8. Bernard Bloch and George L. Trager, *Outline of Linguistic Analysis,* Linguistic Society of America (Baltimore, MD: Waverley Press, 1942), reprinted in 1948.

and facial expressions we would communicate like lifeless robots. Anybody who has ever watched an infant acquire language knows that gesturing, pointing, and making facial grimaces can be highly communicative in a large number of highly specific situations.[9]

If it is true—as generally agreed upon by anthroposophists—that individual evolution or "ontogenesis" tends to recapitulate general human evolution or "philogenesis," a point first made by the German biologist-philosopher Ernst Haeckel, it makes sense to imagine that ancient humanity communicated as much with gestures as it did with "vocal noises"—that is, with the spoken word.

Nor did this possibility go unnoticed. The great eighteenth century philosopher and professor of jurisprudence, Giambattista Vico, Italy's Goethe, expressly suggested that early human communication in the Divine Age was *gestural.* (Vico spoke of a "Divine Age," a "Heroic Age," a "Human Age" and an "Age of Chaos" which tend to repeat themselves cyclically.)[10] This view shows an awareness of the great *yugas* of Indian philosophy—also acknowledged by the early theosophists and later by anthroposophy, *mutatis mutandis.*

If human communication was indeed originally gestural, then what gesture one made in order to say something could not have been a matter of an "arbitrary choice" in today's sense. Think of the beckoning motion, "come toward me;" the halting

---

9. See Michael A.K. Halliday, *Learning How to Mean* (London: Edward Arnold, 1975).
10. Giambattista Vico, *La szienza nuova* [The new science], Max Fisch and Eugen Bär trans. (Cornell University Press, 1983). This is not the right place to go into Vico's philosophy in depth, although numerous fruitful comparisons exist between Vico's thought, Goethe's philosophy of life, and many insights offered by Rudolf Steiner in the anthroposophical literature.

This is a subject which deserves detailed investigation in the not too distant future.

motion, "stop;" the waving motion, "let us go;" the kneeling position in prayer; the posture of hands extended upward to greet the rising sun; the hands held out in a gesture of healing or blessing. We may think of nature, too, as communicating through what we may call "gestures"—lightning as an expression of the "wrath of heaven" and a rainbow as a sign of peace. In this sense, Egyptian tomb painting and the comparatively static nature of Egyptian art may also be thought of as gestural and symbolic. But once modern language had developed, gesturing remained only as a secondary means of communication, including all the familiar gestures we may make ranging from the sublime—as in church, for instance—to the mundane.

At a stage of development closer to our own, however, humanity learned to call actions, things and notions by NAMES (sounds) formed by the vocal chords and the articulatory organs inside the oral cavity.

The "arbitrariness" of the relationship between CONCEPT and SOUND SEQUENCE is commonplace to anyone who has ever learned a foreign language. Is the concept of a 'dog' better expressed as *dog* (as in English) or better as *Hund* (as in German), or perhaps better yet as *sobaka* in Russian or *chien* in French? Perhaps, as Steiner suggests, the difference between different words describing the same object in different languages is ascribable to the fact that different aspects of the object are being stressed. Nevertheless, the moment you do not call a dog 'bow-wow' or some other sound that tries to imitate a dog's barking, you have accepted the inescapable fact that today, 2,000 years after Christ walked the earth, the relationship between concepts and sound sequences certainly seems "arbitrary."

This was not always so. The phenomenon of ONOMATOPOEIA proves, internationally, that certain sounds express certain ideas better than others. The sounds *nyam-nyam,* due to the palatal nature of /y/ and the bilabial nature of /m/ stand in a closer relation to 'eating' and 'that tastes good' than to 'anger' and 'killing'; *hit, strike,* on the other hand, due to the voiceless /t/,/s/, and /k/ sounds imitate better the harshness of a violent blow.

But just as a child outgrows the available sounds to embed its sensations in sound, so humanity, too, outgrew the available sound inventory for its more abstract notions. Languages have therefore evolved an ABSTRACT VOCABULARY. We use words as nouns such as *situation, likelihood, plausibility, inventory, circumnavigation, apprehension, modus operandi* and *serendipity* along with verbs such as *approximate, rationalize, quantify, relinquish* and the like alongside the older monosyllabic Anglo-Saxon ones such as *sit, run, swim, eat, love, die,* etc.

The science of linguistics in the West is commonly thought of as being coeval with the brothers Wilhelm and Jakob Grimm who, starting in 1812 and 1820, began to collect and compare fairy tales in the Germanic languages and found that they resembled each other a great deal.

When Jakob Grimm extended this finding to the Germanic languages as a group, comparing it with Latin and Greek, he found that the Germanic family, in its entirety, differed from Greek and Latin (and also Sanskrit which was studied later) in a systematic way.

Thus where Germanic had /f/, /θ/ and /h/ (from an earlier /x/), Latin and Greek had /p/, /t/, and /k/, as in these examples:

GERMANIC: GREEK/LATIN:

A/1. father (Eng.) : At. *pater,* Gk. *pater* <IE *$p\bar{\partial}t\bar{e}r$
      Vater (Ger.)([v] = /f/)
      foot, Fuß   : Lat. *pes- ped(al, -estrian),* Gk.
                      pod(iatrist) <IE *ped*
      fire, Feuer : Gk. *pyr-(omaniac)* <IE *$p\bar{u}r$*
      for, für   : Lat. *per* <*IE* *per*

five, fünf   :   Gk. penta(gon), [Lat. *quinque* goes
                      back to an older IE ***pemkwe***]
fee, Vieh   :   Lat. *pecu* 'cattle' <IE ***pek***

A/2.   three, drei :   Lat. *tres,* Gk. *tri-* Skt. *trayas* <IE ***tri***
       thumb, Daume :   Lat. *tumēre* 'to swell' <IE ***tum***
       thorp, Dorf :   Lat. *turba,* <IE ***tref***

A/3.   heart, Herz :   Lat. *cord(ial),* Gk. *kardi(ogram)* <IE
                        kerd
       hound, Hund :   Lat. *canis,* Gk. *kuon (cyn-ical* 'dog-
                        like') <IE ***kuon***
       hundred, hundert :   Lat. *cent,* Gk. *(he)-katon* (Latin [c]
                        = /k/) <IE ***kmtóm***

This has become known as Grimm's Law. Steiner was, of
course, very much aware of it, and draws many of his examples
from it. Indeed, in a most interesting and insightful way, he
even extends Grimm's two-step process to include a three step
process. Unfortunately, however, the technical complexities
required to explain and comment upon this from the perspec-
tive of contemporary linguistics would take us too far afield
and extend this Afterword beyond its reasonable bounds.

   In Grimm's Law, as depicted above, what Sets A/1, A/2 and
A/3 indicate is called FRICATIVIZATION, i.e. the fact that Greek
and Latin /p/, /t/, and /k/ correspond to the Germanic frica-
tives /f/, /θ/ and /h/ (from an earlier /x/).

   At the same time Grimm noticed that Indo-European must
have had a separate set of sounds, known as VOICED ASPIRATE
STOPS which, in turn, became voiced but unaspirated stops in
Germanic.

Thus we have:

B/1.   brother, Bruder : Lat. *frater,* Skt. *bhrāta* <IE ***bhratēr***
      beaver : Lat. *fiber,* <IE ***bhibhru***
      blow, blasen : Lat. *flāre,* <IE ***bhlē-***
      break, brechen : Lat. *fra(n)go (fragile)* <IE ***bhreg-***
      bake, backen : Gk. *phōgein* 'bake' <IE ***bhəg-***

B/2.   daughter, Tochter : Gk. *thygater,* Skt. *dhϴta* <IE
                           dhug(h)tēr
      door, Tür :   Lat. *foris* 'door', Rus. *dver'* <IE
                           dhwer
      do, tun : Gk. *the-* 'place, do' <IE ***dhē-***
      dough :   Lat. *fi(n)gere* 'to mold' <IE
                  dheigh-

B/3.   yard, EO geard,
      Garten :   Lat. *hortus (horticulture)* <IE
                ghordho-
      guest, Gast : Lat. *hostis,* <IE ***ghosti-***
      gall : Gk. *cholē* (whence *cholera*) <IE
                ghol-
      get : Lat. *(pre)he(n)dere* 'to take, get' <IE
      ghed-

Lastly, there was also a voiced stop series in Indo-European that, in turn, became voiceless in Germanic (/b/, /d/, /g/ > /p/, /t/, and /k/:

C/1.   hemp, O. Ice. hampr : Gk. *kannabis* <IE ***kanapos***
      thorp, Dorf : Lat. *turba* <IE ***terf***
      (as in *Halethorp, Winthrop*)

C/2.   tooth, Zahn : Lat. *dent-(al,ist),* Gk. *o-dont* <IE
               dent-

two, zwei	:	Lat. *duo,* Skt. *dvayā-* <IE ***dwō***
ten, zehn	:	Lat: *dec-(imal),* Gk. *deka* <IE ***dekm̥***
eat, essen	:	Lat. *edere* <IE ***ed-***
tame, zahm	:	Lat. *domāre (domesticated)* <IE ***dem***
tree	:	Gk. *drūs* 'oak', Rus. *derevo* <IE ***drew-***

C/3.	acre	:	Lat. *ager-agri(culture)* <IE ***agro-***
	knee, Knie	:	Lat. *genu-(flect)* <IE ***gen-***
	Gwen(dolyn), queen	:	Gk. *gyne-(cology)* <IE ***gwen***
	corn, Korn	:	Lat. *granum* <IE ***grəno-***
	know, can, kennen	:	Lat. *(g)noscere* <IE ***gno-***

Linguistics teaches that "sounds change." It traces as closely as possible the way language sounds or phonemes change, but linguists do not comment on the reason or the "feeling" this creates.

Unlike Steiner's approach to language, linguistics is in no position to ask WHY THESE CHANGES HAVE OCCURRED and to what, if any, soul or consciousness qualities they correspond. Linguistics can trace the WHAT of language change, but hardly the WHY of it. It seems to linguists that Germanic hasn't lost very much at all: Indo-European had /*p/, /*t/, /*k/; /*b/, /*d/, /*g/ and /*bh/, /*dh/, /*gh/ (these being reconstructed sounds based on the extant evidence of Greek, Latin and Sanskrit) with Germanic having received back /f/, /θ/ and /h/ from the first set; /p/, /t/, /k/ from the second; and /b/, /d/ and /g/ from the last. In other words *IE had a voiceless stop series, which was fricativized in Germanic, but instead Germanic got a voiceless stop series back from the *IE voiced series, and, whereas the *IE aspirated series loses its /h/ and deaspirates in Germanic, such 'aspiration' is regained in Germanic by the first shift, in which the voiceless stops fricativize, that is, receive an /h/-like quality.

It is a systematic turn-around of three separate changes occurring at three separate times, since if the changes had all occurred at the same time, we would have no words today such as *brother, daughter* and *goose;* they would have to be **prother, *taughter, *koose,* respectively, since /b/, /d/, and /g/ would have gone to /p/, /t/, and /k/. "Here is proof," linguists say, somewhat in the style of Sherlock Holmes and Hercule Poirot, "that these words come from *IE /*bh/, /*dh/, and /*gh/!"

By the same Holmesian reasoning, our words today that have /p/, /t/, and /k/ in them, cannot possibly come from original *IE /*p/, /*t/ and /*k/ sounds, for if they had, they would have changed into /f/, /θ/ and /h/ and would sound like **hemf, *thorf, *ahre, *hnee, *θooth, *θen,* instead if *hemp, thorp, acre, knee, tooth* and *ten.* Another way of putting this is that these changes could have eaten each other up, if they had occurred in the wrong order in time—from our point of view, that is.

Linguistics calls this RELATIVE CHRONOLOGY and must satisfy itself with a statement of facts as they are available by logical reconstructions and calculus.

Steiner characterizes German as having "metamorphosed beyond" English and Dutch. From Indo-European /d/ (as in Latin *decem* 'ten') the German language (by the second High German consonant shift) formed the word *zehn* which has an initial /ts/ affricate in place of the English /t/. Thus we have *IE /d/ > English /t/ > German /z/ = [ts].

In Steiner's view of the situation this further consonant change is viewable as a "metamorphosis" beyond English and Dutch. Steiner also says that the additional changes that occurred made German more, as it were "spiritualized"; more able to describe spiritual realities, and eventually more abstract. He says that, a hundred years before his time, the "language genius" of German was still more creative but that by the twentieth century it became abstract. He says that German word order is quite free and that, in comparison, "Western languages" speak in stereotypes. It seems to me that whereas French, for instance, is hard to play with, the English language, by virtue of its vast vocabulary, has remained remarkably elastic and prone to innovation. (It is interesting to note that the ability of English to renew itself and always come up with new terms is heavily tied to the industrial civilization of the United States and to the innumerable brand names and technical terms that low and high tech industry has created. We are not coining Anglo-Saxon words of the *snow, man, woman, child* type, but Latinate and Hellenistic ones such as *transceiver, transduct, extra-vehicular activity [or EVA], Lunar Orbit Rendezvous [or LOR],* etc. It is as if a second, computer-oriented "language genius" were at work at NASA and in the offices of the Madison Avenue motivational researchers.)

Steiner's remark about the abstractness of German already in the 19th century rings true—certainly, the language of the most complicated modern philosophy has been German. Also, German, by borrowing far fewer Romance loan words than English, had to express its abstract ideas by combining Germanic morphemes. Thus we have *Begriff* from *greifen* 'grasp' for 'concept', *Zusammenhang* from 'together' and 'hang' for 'connection', and so on. I will turn to Steiner's view on semantic change below.

Before I do so, however, I must make one last comment.

Steiner considers German *Mutter* 'mother' to be somehow more "ancient" than Latin *mater,* Greek *mētēr,* or Sanskrit *māta.* This is because, in his own spiritual investigation, Steiner perceives the sound /u/ as more primordial.

As stated above, linguistics cannot agree or disagree with this. All one can say is that Steiner is talking about something else, something on a different plane which is not fathomable by dialectical consciousness. If it had anything to say at all, linguistics would have to say that modern German *Mutter* and English *mother* are both considerably "younger" formations than either the Greek, Latin or Sanskrit, and that the Indo-European reconstruction for 'mother' was **māter.* Out of the thirty Indo-European languages cited by Buck only Old High German and Middle High German have an /u/ sound in *muodar* and *muoder,* respectively.[11] The logic-based linguistic evidence would seem to indicate, then, that any German form with an /u/ is a relatively recent Germanic innovation not shared by the other coeval languages and by none of the attested ancient ones.

Whence this feeling on Steiner's part, then, that German is the closest to the true sound for 'mother' because of the /u/ sound?

As the creator of the new art of Eurythmy, Steiner used his clairvoyant capabilities to perceive how the gestures and movements of the human being could express the living reality of vowels and consonants. A spiritual scientist, he had investigated the supersensible nature underlying language as we know it. And as a consequence of such researches, he was able to speak in ways inaccessible to one without his developed faculties.

These may be entirely valid in their own right. In other words, the German word *Mutter,* due to its /u/ sound, may be "truer" to the spiritual reality than any other Indo-European word for 'mother.' What this, however, does NOT mean is that other female speakers of Indo-European languages had somehow less love for their children or that German is older or in any sense "purer" than Persian, Sanskrit, Latin, Greek, etc., nor is Steiner suggesting anything of the kind.

This needs to be made absolutely clear above all because one of anthroposophy's most vulnerable points is a certain Germanocentrism. Well-read anthroposophists are aware, of course, that

11. Carl Darling Buck, *A Dictionary of Selected Synonyms in the Principal Indo-European Languages* (University of Chicago Press, 1949), paperback edition 1988.

Steiner maintains in several places that whereas the initiation language of antiquity was Classical Greek, the modern language of initiation is German. There is a certain justification for such a view, if we look at the extant body of philosophy in antiquity and in modern times. From Thales and Anaximandros to Plato and Aristotle and beyond, ancient philosophy—in the West—was indeed written in Greek, and modern philosophy from Kant, Fichte, Hegel, Schelling, Feuerbach, Marx, Schopenhauer and Nietzsche, Husserl, Heidegger and Steiner, in German.

Nor can we, as linguists, have the least idea what language might have been like in most ancient times, before historical records. Linguistics can go no farther than 2000 B.C. at best. The oldest Vedic texts are dated 1200 B.C., and only after World War II did Ventris and Chadwick succeed in England in breaking the code of 'Linear B' found on Crete, which is a few hundred years older and is considered as imported from peninsular Mycaenaean Greek to the island of Crete.

III.

STEINER ON SEMANTIC CHANGE

It is in the area of semantic change—the changes that occur in the meaning of a word throughout time—that Steiner's ingenuity reveals itself at its best. He has correctly anticipated one of the most important insights of twentieth century scholarship and that is the observation of the fact that meaning change progresses from the concrete towards the abstract with practically no exceptions.[12] (This is, alas, not to say that all practicing linguists understand or appreciate this point. If they did, we would be closer to closing the gap between academic linguistics and spiritual science.)

All of Steiner's examples on this subject are brilliant and true, with just a couple of minor unchecked improvisations which I will point out below.

The English *lord* does indeed derive from 'loaf-ward' [he who guards the bread or livelihood of a group] and *lady* does indeed derive from 'loaf-kneader' [she who prepares the food]. German *stolz* 'proud' does indeed derive from *stellen-(Ge)stalt* 'stood somewhere' and the expression *Hagestalt* 'confirmed bachelor' does indeed mean 'he who has been stood in the hedge [having inherited nothing else as the younger brother and who is therefore too poor to marry]'. Indeed, even entirely abstract motions, such as the word *abstract* itself, derive from physical images such as *ab-* 'away' and *traho, trahere, traxi, tractus* 'to pull'. Thus, *abstract* from *abstractus* means 'that which has been pulled further away, carried off to a distance'.

What was perhaps somewhat less clear in 1920 and 1925 than today is the enormously increased role of the English language in the ever accelerating spread and scope of world events.

Everything that Steiner said to the assembled Waldorf teachers about language, using German as his example, would seem to fit English even more. The translators are, of course, aware of this and many helpful remarks as interjections in parentheses prove their awareness.

If any language in the history of the world shows the organic amalgamation of formerly separate "national geniuses"—linguists would say "semantic and grammatical structures"—it is English. Whatever amount of Southern European, Christianity-based expressions—from Latin via French—German may

---

12. See Heinz Kronasser, *Handbuch der Semasiologie* (Heidelberg: Akademischer Verlag, 1952). Also on the same subject see Adam Makkai *Idiom Structure in English* (The Hague: Mouton, 1972) in which the development from the concrete to the abstract is documented in great detail.

have assimilated (e.g. *predigen* 'to preach' from Latin *predicāre*), *segen* 'to bless' from *signum* 'a sign,' the number of these is dwarfed by the massive onslaught that English had to assimilate in the wake of the Norman conquest of 1066.

It has often been remarked that if an extra-terrestrial visitor had to make a report on the English language by scanning the printed literature, the report would state that Great Britain, Canada, the United States, Australia and New Zealand, plus a large number of countries from India to Kenya where English is a second joint official language due to the colonial past, speak a neo-Romance language closely related to Spanish, French, Italian, Portuguese and Rumanian with some sort of an archaic residue that distantly resembles German and the other Germanic languages.

This is no exaggeration. The reader is encouraged to try to translate into "pure Germanic English" common expressions such as *anthroposophy, anthropology, geology, geography, gynecology, podiatrist, solar eclipse, lunar eclipse, lunation, situation, abandon*—to mention just a few. It can be done, but the results look funny. The fact of the matter is that the Graeco-Latin-Romance layer of English lexis carries the notions of "professionalism" and "reliability," while the Anglo-Saxon-Germanic translations smack of amateurism and of a rough-hewn, home-spun nature.

Steiner's general insight that the abstract vocabulary of today evolved out of concrete experiences of the past can perhaps be best illustrated with the Indo-European root **wed*. Its extant cognates (not mentioned by Steiner) are *Veda* in Sanskrit, *video, vidēre, vīdi, vīsus* 'to see' in Latin, *wit* 'intelligence' and *witness* 'some one who knows something because he or she has seen it'. The second Germanic consonant shift changed the /t/ present in English and the /d/ present in Sanskrit and Latin into /s/ or / ß/ as in *wissen* 'to know', *ich weiß, du weißt, er weiß, die Wissenschaft* 'science'.

Why is this such a telling example?

Because if 'to see' and 'to know' are cognate—and they demonstrably are—the modern English saying *I see what you mean* meaning "I understand your point" makes perfect sense, even if it is said by a blind person. The original faculty of "sight" need not have been purely physical, as it is today for most human beings in the waking state of logical consciousness. Originally, perhaps, one also "saw" things in clairvoyance, a state of consciousness distantly and distortedly related to today's dream-consciousness.

The contemporary, purely descriptive semantic spread of this etymon proves Steiner's point in a way that even the most sceptical, behavioristic-materialistic linguist would have to concede the point. *Insight* has precious little to do with the physical ability to look into a hidden place with some sort of a mechanical device such as a telescope —it much rather refers to "sudden comprehension," to the "ability to perceive a previously hidden connection between two things or ideas."

We also say *seeing is believing.* The task facing the scientific linguist is to believe that the ancients saw things such as the human aura. Anthropologically interested linguists may tolerate the concept of a 'human aura,' for instance among the Yaqui Indians of the Sonora desert, but much less in the class room of a North American University.

IV.
IDIOMATICITY AS THE BEST WAY TO UNDERSTAND
RUDOLF STEINER'S VIEW OF LANGUAGE

An idiom is a fixed expression whose meaning does not logically derive from the sum of its parts and which projects a particular image. I have written a major book on the subject, based on a Yale Ph.D., and have edited several dictionaries of idioms.[13]

As anybody fluent in English will agree, idiomatic expressions are livelier and more popular than the pedantic paraphrases one can assign to them in a dictionary. The English language is perhaps one of the very richest in idioms. The recent edition of the *Dictionary of American English Idioms* mentioned in the above footnote has well over 8,000 entries in it.

As speakers of English, we much prefer saying *he gave up* to 'he ceased trying'; we rather say *John always gives in* instead of 'he tends to surrender his will'. *My car gave out on me* is much preferred to the pedantic 'it stopped functioning' and we rather say *why bring up that unpleasant subject* to 'why mention it'. Each of the idioms involved is the result of a semantic force alive in English today to say with short Anglo-Saxon words what would otherwise require a lengthy, poly-syllabic Franco-Latin or Hellenistic paraphrase. The short Anglo-Saxon words invariably create an image. *He threw in the towel* allows you to see how someone quits a fight—you can see the gesture of the wet towel hitting the floor and the defeated boxer or wrestler leaving in disgust.

All of these were live imaginations in the not-too-distant past of English. Yet it is unfortunately true that, as Steiner implies throughout, these idioms tend to rigidify into schemata that eventually stand in the way of original thought. Too many people use idiomatic speech without realizing what the underlying image is or was. One can see this in fluent English language users who weren't born in the United States. They can easily say *he'll never get to first base* and *he's got two strikes against*

---

13. See Makkai *Idiom Structure in English,* op. cit., as well as *A Dictionary of American English Idioms,* 3rd revised and updated edition (Hauppauge, N.Y.: Barron's Educational Series, 1995).

him meaning 'he'll never succeed in getting anywhere' and 'he is out if he makes one more mistake' without realizing what these expressions refer to in the game of baseball. People ape expressions such as *that will put the icing on the cake* meaning 'that will put the finishing touch or crown on a given job' while having never iced a cake in a kitchen themselves.

Thus for human consciousness the idiom is a double-edged sword. In positive terms, it is an image, still alive in many places, that replaces a Latinate or Hellenistic abstraction. On the negative side, it can become a lifeless cliché, mimed and aped by people under peer pressure who actually do not have an image in mind at all.

Steiner shows great insight into what linguistics calls IRRE-VERSIBLE BINOMIALS. These include expressions such as *part and parcel, drawn and quartered, nip and tuck, touch and go,* and literally hundreds of others. Steiner is correct in pointing out that such doublets arise because speakers were not satisfied either with the first word or with the second by itself, so they sought an interim solution and came up with the doublet. (The reason linguists call them 'irreversible' is that they always go in the order given. We do not say *parcel and part,* for instance.)

One more remark about the development of the 'Ego' and verb conjugation: Steiner writes that a paradigm such as *amo, amas, amat, amamus, amatis, amant*—a typical Latin conjugation—meaning 'I love, thou lovest, he/she/ loves, we love, you (pl.) love, they love' indicates a period in our development when the sense of individuality was less developed. Since it was still weak, people did not express it as the separate word 'I', 'You', 'He/She', etc., but added it as a suffix to the verb. Later, when the 'I' became stronger, more "incarnated" in humans, the inflectional endings gradually dropped off and people began expressing the person that was meant. Thus today in English we have *I love, YOU love, HE/SHE loves, WE love, YOU love, THEY love.*

This is certainly well worth considering.

Standard linguistics does not consider the Ego or I in anthroposophical terms—most linguists would at best think of Sigmund Freud's trichotomy of the Super-Ego, the Ego and the Id and most would probably even regard these as inessential for a scientific linguistics. [In fact, the field of psycholinguistics has not yet even begun to look at the unconscious. Very few linguists are concerned with phenomena such as the so-called Freudian slip. However, certain permutations of the three Freudian ego-states have shown up in Transactional Psychoanalysis in which we speak of a Parental, and Adult, and Child-like Ego-state.[14] These can, at least, offer some explanation as to why some people act superior and judgmental (parental), adequate and matter-of-fact (adult) or submissive and playful, or creative (child-like). But grammar has no explanation for the "tones of voice" carried by these emotional states.] To say, then, that the I was less incarnated in ancient humanity than in modern people, goes far beyond the most daring statement that even Carl Jung might have made, whose idea of the 'collective unconscious' is still ridiculed by many.

Standard linguistics explains—or tries to explain—the gradual loss of personal endings on verbs due to phonological conditioning. The accent moved to the front; the last syllable was murmured and, eventually, forgotten. French still writes many of them but doesn't pronounce them.

---

14. See Eric Berne *Games People Play* (New York: Grove Press, 1966). Also compare T.A. Harris, *I'm OK—You're OK* (New York: Harper & Row, 1967). In my book *Ecolinguistics* (London: Pinter Publishers and Budapest: Akadémiai kiadó, 1993), I devoted a separate chapter to the distortions of logic (Chapter #4) preceded by a chapter (Chapter #2) on the relationship of linguistics to its mother discipline, anthropology, which, if properly expanded, might be able to absorb individual as well as social psychology which would be a healthy step toward an understanding of real speech.

Generally, everything Steiner posits an inner reason for, materialistic modern scholarship seeks to explain by offering some exterior reason. Steiner views 'Umlaut' [the changing of singular into plural by vowel change in German and English] as in *man: men; woman: women; goose: geese; foot: feet;* or German *Mann: Männer; Vater: Väter; Mutter: Mütter; Bruder: Brüder* as involving a "dulling" of the pure sound to a murky one—a movement paralleling the shift in attention from a concretely observed fact or sensation to something that cannot be so closely observed. Standard linguistics, once more, offers an external explanation and insists that in pre-Old English, for instance, the dative of *goose* was *gōsi* and that it was this final /i/ sound that affected the long /ē/ and caused it to change into a long /ō/ written *-ee-* which, then, after the Great Vowel Shift [between 1,400 and 1,500] became pronounced /iy/ as in today's pronunciation /giys/.

V.

LINGUISTICS AS THE "CONSCIOUSNESS SOUL"
DISCIPLINE *PAR EXCELLENCE*

Speculation about language is as old as humanity itself.

Plato discussed it; Dante wrote about it. In ancient India, the grammarian Panini wrote the world's most complete grammar to this day on Sanskrit in 500 B.C. Unfortunately, the West only discovered it in the nineteenth century.

In ancient China there were many excellent dictionaries, far antedating the thesaurus concept that was invented in the West in England in the nineteenth century by Roget. The subject is so complex and so multifarious that a comprehensive history of linguistics, in spite of many valiant attempts, is still missing.

Modern linguistics, as we know it, was a German invention and it started, as indicated above, with the Brothers Grimm around 1812. The field was quite understandably, somewhat German-centered. Indo-European itself was known as Indo-Germanic. Scholars were unaware of the fact that the Comparative Method was, in fact, invented by a Hungarian Jesuit in the later eighteenth century who compared Hungarian (or Magyar) to Lappish.[15]

The German linguistics of the nineteenth century was a primarily philologically based enterprise. Its practitioners were concerned primarily with Latin and Greek; readings and interpretations of the *Iliad* and the *Odyssey* were normal fare besides the Latin classics. Neither should we forget that the excavation of Troy and Mycenae were German contributions to archeology and to our understanding of our common European and Near Eastern heritage.[16] Yet the discovery of Sanskrit as an integral part of Indo-European was a British contribution.[17]

---

15. Sámuel Gyarmathi (1751–1830): *Affinitas linguae Hungaricae cum linguis Fennicae originis grammatice demonstrata* [A Grammatical Demonstration of the Affinity of the Hungarian Language with languages of Finnish Origin], Göttingen, 1799; this was actually preceded by the work of János Sajnovics (1753–1785) who published his book on a similar topic in 1770: *Demonstratio Idioma Ungarorum et Lapponum idem esse* [A Demonstration that the Language of the Hungarians and the Lapps is the Same].

16. Heinrich N. Schliemann (1822–1890) was the excavator of Troy and of Mycaenae. See J. Hermann, *Heinrich Schliemann, Wegbereiter einer neuen Wissenschaft*, 1974.

17. Sir William Jones (1746–1794) read his famous statement in the Royal Asiatic Society about the striking relationship between Greek, Latin and Sanskrit many years before the Brothers Grimm started their comparative work in Germany. The actual relevance of Sanskrit, however, was not fully appreciated until the middle of the nineteenth century, when some of the most outstanding Indo-Europeanists who also knew Sanskrit were German scholars, such as Böhtlingk, Bopp, Osthoff, Leskien, Brugmann, etc. The most important Sanskritist in the English speaking world during this period was William Dwight Whitney (1827–1894)

The French, too, have been prominent in Indo-European studies. The names of Ferdinand De Saussure (1857–1913), and Antoine Meillet (1866–1936) must be mentioned in this regard (with De Saussure having been a Francophone Swiss).

It is generally held that De Saussure is the father of modern linguistics. What do we mean by this? It is in the collected lectures by De Saussure entitled *Cours de linguistique générale* [A Course in General Linguistics] (several English translations exist; the standard one by Wade Baskin is now supplanted by that of Roy Harris) that the famous principle of the arbitrariness of the relationship between the 'signifier' and the 'signified' is expressed for the first time. Whereas Plato had already considered the matter in antiquity and decided that words came by their sounds and their meanings more by convention or *nomos* than by their nature or *physis*,[18] no scientific statement of world-wide acceptance was made on this matter before De Saussure.

In De Saussure's view the LINGUISTIC SIGN is a double-bodied entity consisting of a 'concept' or the 'signified' (in French *le signifié*) and a 'sound sequence' known as the 'signifier' (*in French le signifiant*.) The two form an inseparable entity: You can take away the one only at the expense of removing the other as well. If you imagine a 'cat' as the concept and think of the various names various languages call the same animal from German *Katze*

Whitney was an advanced graduate student still in his early twenties, was sent from Yale to Germany to study with Böhtlingk in Göttingen by Professor Edward Salisbury who, upon Whitney's return to Yale, resigned his chair and endowed a chair for Indo-European studies at Yale with Whitney as its first holder. Yale University has been one the world's leading centers for Indo-European studies internationally and in the USA in particular, with scholars such as Prokosch, Sturtevant, Edgerton, Bloomfield, Bloch, Dyen, Thieme, Tedesco, Cowgill and Insler in the 20th century.

18. See Francis P. Dinneen *An Introduction to General Linguistics* (New York: Holt Rinehart & Winston, 1967), in which he carefully explains the ancient "physis-nomos" controversy in Plato's days.

through English *cat* to French *chat* and Russian *koška,* you will readily see that it is futile to think that the one sound sequence is somewhat more "feline" or cat-like than any one of the others.

We are, therefore, in the twentieth century and beyond, in the state of consciousness where arbitrariness prevails as the primary force that holds a concept and its expression together.

We live in a daytime, waking, logical mode of object-consciousness but, since we are in contact with foreign languages, we may have all had experiences of finding out what words can stand for in a language we do not know.

Let us consider a brief set of words from Indonesian or 'Bahasa Indonesia' the official language of over 200 million people in the Republic of Indonesia, a country of thousands of islands. (If you know the language skip this paragraph; if you do not, try to guess what the words mean and DO NOT rush to an Indonesian dictionary):

1. anjing   2. kuching   3. kerbau   4. saya   5. minum
6. susu   7. kopi   8. tidak   9. akan   10. sekarang
11. silakan   12. duduk   13. selamat   14. pagi   15. malam
16. tuan   17. sudah   18. memakan   19. nasi   20. bukan
21. kawin   22. belum   23. didalam   24. apa   25. daripada

From this set of words you can construct the following sentences (in the right order, of course): (1) Have you had your meal (eaten yet), Sir? (2) I will not drink milk. (3) Please have a seat. (4) Good morning, Sir! (5) Good evening, Sir! (6) Are you married yet, Sir? (7) Yes, I am already (married). (8) No, I am not yet (married). (9) I will/want to drink coffee. [19]

---

19. 1. *Tuan sudah memakan nasi?* 2. *Saya tidak akan minum susu.* 3. *Silakan duduk.* 4. *Selemat pagi, Tuan!* 5. *Selemat malam, Tuan!* 6. *Tuan sudah kawin?* 7. *Sudah.* 8. *Belum.* 9. *Saya akan minum kopi.*

What are the odds that, without knowing which word means what, a person not knowing Indonesian will be able to produce these sentences? You will agree, I believe, that they are infinitesimally small. Why were certain words on this twenty-five word list not used in the making of the nine Indonesian sentences? What is the meaning of the words *anjing, kuching* and *kerbau?*[20]

As this short exercise of looking at an unfamiliar language will indicate, arbitrariness stares us in the face first and foremost when we are dealing with a language we do not know. Once the instructor or our new neighbors have told us what certain words mean, the arbitrariness of the new words gradually fades away and we develop a feeling of naturalness for them. After a year or two in Indonesia, if some one tries to tell us that *kuching* means 'water buffalo', we will probably vigorously defend the meaning 'cat' with as much passion as if some one were trying to tell us that *sassafras* means 'gold bullion'. Arbitrariness in the concept-sound relationship is part and parcel of the human condition in the fifth culture of the fifth post-Atlantian epoch.

But, as anthroposophy tells us, this was not always the case.

Rudolf Steiner reminds us that the spoken word used to have creative power. When God said 'let there be light', light came into being by the power of this word. And, certainly, the Elohim, mentioned in the Old Testament, could use the power of their creative words. Similarly, when Christ Jesus says to the paralyzed man "gather up thy bed and walk" He uses the Power of the Word as no one alive today can, but He does so in accordance with the destiny of each specific person He chooses to cure. The words of the Elohim and of Christ Jesus had a special power all their own, but this power was not used out of context—quite the contrary. The Elohim and Christ Jesus used their Words carefully.

---

20. They are 'dog', 'cat' and 'water buffalo', respectively.

This situation resembles, if only vaguely, the "arbitrariness" of a foreign word. The context of Indonesian society creates a climate on the Indonesian islands in which *kuching* means 'cat' and not 'dog' or 'water buffalo'. The foreigner who can discover this fact and use these words in wise accordance with their use by the Indonesians, in a sense accepts the 'karma' of these words and inwardly agrees to accept them as they are used by the native speakers. If this were not so, nobody could ever become fluent in a second language and speak it with any manner of believability. In writing these lines in English, a second language to me, I no longer fight the battle of the "arbitrariness" issue that English words used to confront me with when I first came to the United States from Hungary at the age of twenty-one. The once very real arbitrariness of *apple, pear, spoon* and *fork* is now replaced by confidence that these sounds are right for these concepts —in other words they have become second nature to me, just as are their Hungarian equivalents *alma, körte, kanál* and *villa* which will undoubtedly sound arbitrary to someone who knows no Hungarian. But something downright magical has occurred by my conquering my own resistance to the words that were once foreign to me—whether in Indonesian or in English—and this ability to overcome the resistance to what seemed "arbitrary" has enabled me to gain membership in the new speech community of English speakers.

It is as if a bit of the karma of the English language had rubbed off on me, a newcomer to this great tongue.

But this is still mini-magic and rather mundane. We still cannot make water flow out of a rock like Moses or Saint Ladislas of Hungary in the early thirteenth century, and we cannot heal the sick by commanding them to "gather up thy bed and walk!" We linguists, no matter how many languages we manage to learn poorly or well, are still captives of daytime waking logical consciousness and our words miserably fail when we want them to work magic.

In fact, the situation is far worse than I have indicated.

Let us consider the problem of pollution for a moment.

We think of the Exxon-Valdez oil spill in Alaska as a major natural disaster, and the Green Movement is actively trying to save the environment in many places the world over. Yet the area of language has sustained pollution levels that far exceed anything in the natural world. Seven decades of Soviet Communism created lies and distortions of mega-Orwellian proportions, not to mention Hitlerian Nazi propaganda and what it did to language.

When the Park Service of Yellowstone Park has to kill hundreds of elk, they talk about "direct reduction." The word 'kill' or 'shoot' sounds too tangible, too bloody. These euphemisms of officialese abound in every sector of modern American society.

In an allegedly free society, such as the United States, three decades after the assassination of President John F. Kennedy we still do not really know what took place. It is possible in 1994 to write thousands of pages in Pentagonese and State Departmentese with very little common sense shining through the pages. We talk about gun control and universal health coverage, but very little actual meaning seeps through the rhetoric and the verbiage.

At the same time, we have become creators of artificial languages. No self-respecting college student likes to admit if they are computer-illiterate and cannot write a term paper on a personal computer. Supermarket check-out personnel move the merchandise past an electric lens that reads the price coded in bars—no words or figures are used any more. We have developed the intelligence to alter reality around us. The industry brags of this and calls it the long awaited advent of the "information highway" and "virtual reality."

If this trend continues, and the wares become cheaper, generations of young people will grow up who not only will not know what it is like to pick an apple from a tree—chances are they won't even go to a supermarket any more to buy one. Instead, they will touch a place on their television screen and next day some device will deliver some canned apple juice to their door for which they will pay no real cash but punch in a code in their interactive television set and pay with some points that are kept track of by yet another computer.

We have come a dreadfully long way from the time when some one with the power to do so could say "gather up thy bed and walk!"

And yet this is the time in the history of humanity when linguistics became possible on a level of consciousness *where we are beginning to think about thinking.* And that, as Georg Kühlewind would remind us, is a prototypical consciousness soul activity of our time.[21]

Modern linguistics will eventually have to give up its abstract, set-theoretical orientation which claims that it is a great 'mentalist revolution' against the 'Bloomfieldian mechanists' as Chomsky and his followers have been doing. We must learn not to see some kind of real conscious intelligence in computers; we must start using them against Ahrimanic thinking.

Linguistics will have to move closer and closer to an understanding of where our verbal signs come from: The auditory world, the visual-imaginative world, the tactile world, the abstract world of reasoning, or from the forgotten past of atavistic imaginative clairvoyance. Linguistics must stop being a materialistic, abstract enterprise.

---

21. See the following books by Georg Kühlewind: *Stages of Consciousness,* 1984; *Becoming Aware of the Logos,* 1985; and *The Life of the Soul,* 1990 (Hudson, N.Y.: Lindisfarne Press).

Anthroposophists, including those with eurythmy and speech-formation training,—and indeed everyone—would do well to learn a bit of articulatory and acoustic phonetics and phonology for the practical transcription of spoken languages. The study of comparative linguistics [Indo-European or otherwise] can only help in telling apart false cognates that happen to sound right, from the ones that are harder to ferret out and justify. Terms such as 'Umlaut' and 'Ablaut' have a vast and impressive scholarly literature going back to nineteenth century Germany, and people should be aware of the general layout of the field of linguistics.

I sincerely hope that these remarks will kindle at least a minimal interest in Linguistics among anthroposophists and a similar interest in Rudolf Steiner's immensely interesting philosophy in the general public and among linguists who tend to be far too entrenched in the narrow confines of their logic-bound daily discipline.

ADAM MAKKAI

Professor of Linguistics
University of Illinois at Chicago
Executive Director & Chairman of the Board
of the Linguistic Association of Canada
& The United States [Lacus], Inc.

Further Reading on Speech and Language

By Rudolf Steiner:

The Alphabet. Spring Valley, NY: Mercury Press, 1982.
The Art of Lecturing. Spring Valley, NY: Mercury Press, 1984.
Creative Speech. London: Rudolf Steiner Press, 1978.
Eurythmy as Visible Speech. London: Rudolf Steiner Press, 1985.
Finding and Formulating the Cosmic Word. New York: Anthroposophic Press, 1942.
The Realm of Language. Spring Valley, NY: Mercury Press, 1984.
Speech and Drama. Spring Valley, NY: Anthroposophic Press, 1960.

By Other Authors:

Barfield, Owen. *History in English Words.* London: Faber and Faber, 1926.
Brydon, Bill. *Mother Tongue: English and How It Got That Way.* New York: William Morrow, 1990.
Jespersen, Otto. *The Growth and Structure of the English Language.* New York: Doubleday-Anchor, 1955.
König, Karl. *The First Three Years of the Child.* New York: Anthroposophic Press, 1969.
Lewis, C.S. *Studies in Words.* Cambridge, Mass.: Cambridge University Press, 1961.
Lorenz-Poschmann, Agathe. *Breath, Speech and Therapy.* Spring Valley, NY: Mercury Press, 1982.
Wadler, Arnold. *One Language, Source of All Tongues.* New York: American Press for Art and Science, 1948.

(In German, not yet translated)

Aschenbrenner, Michael. *Das Doppel Autlitz der Sprache.*
Kiersch, Johannes. *Fremndesprachen in der Waldorfschule*, Stutgart: Verlag Freies Geistesleben, 1994.
Lauer, Hans Erhard. *Weltenwort, Menchensprache.* Dornach, Switzerland: Philosophisch-Anthroposophischer Verlag, 1972.
Moll, Ernst. *Die Sprache der Laute.* Stuttgart: Verlag Freies Geistesleben, 1968.

THE FOUNDATIONS
OF WALDORF EDUCATION

THE FIRST FREE WALDORF SCHOOL opened its doors in Stuttgart, Germany, in September, 1919, under the auspices of Emil Molt, the Director of the Waldorf Astoria Cigarette Company and a student of Rudolf Steiner's spiritual science and particularly of Steiner's call for social renewal.

It was only the previous year—amid the social chaos following the end of World War I—that Emil Molt, responding to Steiner's prognosis that truly human change would not be possible unless a sufficient number of people received an education that developed the whole human being, decided to create a school for his workers' children. Conversations with the Minister of Education and with Rudolf Steiner, in early 1919, then led rapidly to the forming of the first school.

Since that time, more than six hundred schools have opened around the globe—from Italy, France, Portugal, Spain, Holland, Belgium, Great Britain, Norway, Finland and Sweden to Russia, Georgia, Poland, Hungary, Rumania, Israel, South Africa, Australia, Brazil, Chile, Peru, Argentina, Japan etc.—making the Waldorf School Movement the largest independent school movement in the world. The United States, Canada, and Mexico alone now have more than 120 schools.

Although each Waldorf school is independent, and although there is a healthy oral tradition going back to the first Waldorf teachers and to Steiner himself, as well as a growing body of secondary literature, the true foundations of the Waldorf method and spirit remain the many lectures that Rudolf Steiner gave on the subject. For five years (1919–24), Rudolf Steiner, while simultaneously working on many other fronts, tirelessly dedicated himself to the dissemination of the idea of Waldorf education. He gave manifold lectures to teachers, parents, the general public, and even the children themselves. New schools were founded. The Movement grew.

While many of Steiner's foundational lectures have been translated and published in the past, some have never appeared in English, and many have been virtually unobtainable for years. To remedy this situation and to establish a coherent basis for Waldorf Education, Anthroposophic Press has decided to publish the complete series of Steiner lectures and writings on education in a uniform series. This series will thus constitute an authoritative foundation for work in educational renewal, for Waldorf teachers, parents, and educators generally.

· · · · · · ·

RUDOLF STEINER'S LECTURES (AND WRITINGS) ON EDUCATION

I. *Allgemeine Menschenkunde als Grundlage der Pädagogik. Pedagogischer Grundkurs,* 14 Lectures Stuttgart, 1919 (GA293). **The Study of Man** (Rudolf Steiner Press, 1981).

II. *Erziehungskunst Methodische-Didaktisches,* 14 Lectures, Stuttgart, 1919 (GA294). **Practical Advice to Teachers** (Rudolf Steiner Press, 1988).

III. *Erziehungskunst,* 15 Discussions, Stuttgart, 1919 (GA 295). **Discussions with Teachers** (Rudolf Steiner Press, 1992).

IV. *Die Erziehungsfrage als soziale Frage,* 6 Lectures, Dornach, 1919 (GA296). **Education as a Social Problem** (Anthroposophic Press, 1969).

V. *Die Waldorf Schule und ihr Geist,* 6 Lectures, Stuttgart and Basel, 1919 (GA 297). **The Spirit of the Waldorf School** (Anthroposophic Press, 1995).

VI. *Rudolf Steiner in der Waldorfschule, Vorträge und Ansprachen,* Stuttgart, 1919–1924 (GA 298). ["**Rudolf Steiner in the Waldorf School—Lectures and Conversations**," Stuttgart, 1919–24].

VII. *Geisteswissenschaftliche Sprachbetrachtungen,* 6 Lectures, Stuttgart, 1919 (GA 299). **The Genius of Language** (Anthroposophic Press, 1995).

VIII. *Konferenzen mit den Lehren der Freien Waldorfschule 1919–1924*, 3 Volumes (GA 300). **Conferences with Teachers** (Steiner Schools Fellowship, 1986, 1987, 1988, 1989).

IX. *Die Erneuerung der Pädagogisch-didaktischen Kunst durch Geisteswissenschaft*, 14 lectures, Basel, 1920 (GA 301). **The Renewal of Education** (Kolisko Archive Publications for Steiner Schools Fellowship Publications, Michael Hall, Forest Row, East Sussex, UK, 1981).

X. *Menschenerkenntnis und Unterrichtsgestaltung*, 8 Lectures, Stuttgart, 1921 (GA 302). **The Supplementary Course—Upper School** (Michael Hall School, Forest Row, 1965) and **Waldorf Education for Adolescence** (Kolisko Archive Publications for Steiner Schools Fellowship Publications, 1980).

XI. *Erziehung und Unterrricht aus Menschenerkenntnis*, 9 Lectures, Stuttgart, 1920, 1922, 1923 (GA302a). The first four Lectures available as **Balance in Teaching** (Mercury Press, 1982); last three lectures as **Deeper Insights into Education** (Anthroposophic Press, 1988).

XII. *Die Gesunder Entwickelung des Menschenwesens,* 16 Lectures, Dornach, 1921–22 (GA303). **Soul Economy and Waldorf Education** (Anthroposophic Press, 1986).

XIII. *Erziehungs- und Unterrichtsmethoden auf Anthroposophische Grundlage*, 9 Public lectures, various cities, 1921–22 (GA304). **Waldorf Education and Anthroposophy I** (Anthroposophic Press, 1995).

XIV. *Anthroposophische Menschenkunde und Pädagogik,* 9 Public lectures, various cities, 1923–24 (GA304a) **Waldorf Education and Anthroposophy II** (Anthroposophic Press, 1995).

XV. *Die geistig-seelischen Grundkräfte der Erziehungskunst*, 12 Lectures, 1 special Lecture, Oxford 1922 (GA 305) **The Spiritual Ground of Education** (Garber Publications, n.d.).

XVI. *Die pädagogisch Praxis vom Gesichtspunkte geisteswissenschaftliche Menschenerkenntnis*, 8 lectures, Dornach, 1923 (GA306). **The Child's Changing Consciousness and Waldorf Education** (Anthroposophic Press, 1988).

XVII. *Gegenwärtiges Geistesleben und Erziehung,* 4 lectures, Ilkeley, 1923 (GA307). *A Modern Art of Education.* (Rudolf Steiner Press, 1981) and *Education and Modern Spiritual Life* (Garber Publications, n.d.).

XVIII. *Die Methodik des Lehrens und die Lebensbedingungen des Erziehens,* 5 Lectures, Stuttgart, 1924 (GA308). *The Essentials of Education* (Rudolf Steiner Press, 1968).

XIX. *Anthroposophische Pädagogik und ihre Voraussentzungen,* 5 Lectures, Bern, 1924 (GA 309). *The Roots of Education* (Rudolf Steiner Press, 1982).

XX. *Der pädagogische Wert der Menschenerkenntnis und der Kulturwert der Pädagogik,* 10 Public lectures, Arnheim, 1924 (GA310). *Human Values in Education* (Rudolf Steiner Press, 1971).

XXI. *Die Kunst des Erziehens aus dem Erfassen der Menschenwesenheit,* 7 lectures, Torquay, 1924 (GA311). *The Kingdom of Childhood* (Anthroposophic Press, 1995).

XXII. *Geisteswissenschaftliche Impulse zur Entwicklung der Physik. Erster naturwissenschaftliche Kurs: Licht, Farbe, Ton—Masse, Elektrizität, Magnetismus,* 10 Lectures, Stuttgart, 1919–20 (GA 320). *The Light Course* (Steiner Schools Fellowship,1977).

XXIII. *Geisteswissenschaftliche Impulse zur Entwickelung der Physik. Zweiter naturwissenschaftliche Kurs: die Wärme auf die Grenze positiver und negativer Materialität,*14 Lectures, Stuttgart, 1920 (GA 321). *The Warmth Course* (Mercury Press, 1988).

XXIV. *Das Verhältnis der verschiedenen naturwissenschaftlichen Gebiete zur Astronomie. Dritter naturwissenschaftliche Kurs: Himmelskunde in Bezeiehung zum Menschen und zur Menschenkunde,* 18 lectures, Stuttgart, 1921 (GA 323). Available in typescript only as "**The Relation of the Diverse Branches of Natural Science to Astronomy.**"

XXV. Miscellaneous.

INDEX

Ablaut, 88

absorbing terms from other
cultures, 17–23, 26, 32–38, 41,
49, 64

abstractness, 24, 36, 45, 56–58, 76,
79

correcting, 93

feeling in the forming of speech,
79

Nachtschlaf (night sleep), 28–29,
74

acre, 53

activity expressed in sounds, 84

Adelung, Johann C., 69

Africa, 46, 82–83

Ahnl (grandmother), 75

albern, 60

alliteration, 58, 63

amusing, awful, artificial, 68

Anglo-Saxon words

dag (dough), 36

for- prefix, 59

ga- prefix, 54, 55–56

guma (human being), 33

hlaifs (bread), 36

maenan (to recite), 35

phonemic changes, 43

rice (powerful and rich), 41

springan (spring), 48

thu, 42

wain, 90

Asia, 46

atavistic clairvoyance, 91–92

attentiveness of students, 93–94

Austrian words, 21, 27, 28–29, 51–
52, 74

bairn, 29

-bar suffix, 30, 50

Beiwacht (keeping watch together),
64

Bible, the, 29–30, 31, 32, 33, 34

Bildung (education), 16

bitter, 70

blessing, concept, 18

bow-wow theory, 28

Braut, Bräutigam, 33

bread, shift in meaning of, 36

bride, bridegroom, 33

brother, brethern, children

Buchstabe (letter of the alphabet),
19–20

cases (syntactic relationship), 79

Celtic element, 38, 40–41, 47

Central European languages, 7, 38–
41, 44, 46, 49

chivalry, age of, 65–67

Christianity, 17–20, 25–26, 47, 51,
61–62

Christmas festival, 18

Christmas Plays from Oberufer
(Harwood), 32

clairvoyance, primitive, 91–92

closing off from outside influences,
39–40

coach, 23

common origin of languages, 38–39

DURING THE LAST TWO DECADES of the nineteenth century the Austrian-born Rudolf Steiner (1861–1925) became a respected and well-published scientific, literary, and philosophical scholar, particularly known for his work on Goethe's scientific writings. After the turn of the century he began to develop his earlier philosophical principles into an approach to methodical research of psychological and spiritual phenomena.

His multifaceted genius has led to innovative and holistic approaches in medicine, science, education (Waldorf schools), special education, philosophy, religion, economics, agriculture (Biodynamic method), architecture, drama, new arts of eurythmy and speech, and other fields. In 1924 he founded the General Anthroposophical Society, which today has branches throughout the world.